FOR STRANGERS PASSING THROUGH

MANY PATHS, MANY MASTERS

דאָס פון וויפעלו

Chassidic Stories

SHOSHANNAH BROMBACHER, Ph.D.

NEW YORK 5779/2020

TotalRecall Publications, Inc.

1103 Middlecreek Friendswood, Texas 77546 281-992-3131 281-482-5390 Fax www.mousegate.com

Copyright © 2021 by: Shoshannah Brombacher Graphics Copyright © 2021 by: Shoshannah Brombacher All rights reserved
ISBN: 9781648830259
UPC: 643977602596
Library of Congress Control Number: 2020942330
Printed and distributed worldwide.

FIRST EDITION
1 2 3 4 5 6 7 8 9 10

A few of the stories in this collection were previously published in a modified version on www.Chabad.org.

Dedicated to my father, Prof. Dr. P.J.Brombacher z"l,
who always inspired me and introduced me to Chassidic stories.

What others say about this book:

Shoshannah Brombacher, a world-class Jewish artist, brings together the best of Chagall and Lieberman (the first Chasidic artist). Her novelty, telling Chasidic stories with highly original and masterful painting and ink and pastel drawings, makes this book truly unique. I encourage everyone to read this book. It will enhance your quality of life.

>**Rabbi Chaim Dalfin, Brooklyn**
>**Author, Historian & Researcher**

ॐ

Dr. Shoshannah Brombacher is not only a gifted artist, but also a talented writer. In her book on chassidic tales, you feel the joy and faith of chassidim that will encourage you to become a better Jew.

>**Rabbi Aaron L Raskin**
>**Cong.Bnai Avraham**
>**Dean BHJA|**
>**heightschabad.com**

ॐ

Shoshannah Brombacher is a uniquely happy and spiritual Jew. More than that, she is a tzaddekes, a holy woman. I want to tune in to whatever she does—whether stories, paintings or both. Three of her paintings grace my living room walls; another three are on the covers of three of my books. I love Jewish art and she is my favorite Jewish artist. I know that she is a charming raconteur and a delightful maggidah (Jewish storyteller) of depth and humor, and I am anxiously looking forward to this book.

>**Maggid Yitzhak Buxbaum,**
>**author of Jewish Spiritual Practices**
>**and The Light and Fire of the Baal Shem Tov.**

A few words from my masterful Maggid teacher, Reb Yitzchak Buxbaum, who taught me the art of Jewish storytelling. Years ago, he contacted me because he was looking for an artist to illustrate the cover of his wonderful book "The Light and Fire of the Baal Shem Tov," which contains (nearly) every known story about the Besht. We became friends and I learned a lot from his courses. He is my great inspiration! Here is what he wrote in his typical "Yitzhak style":

"My name is Yitzhak Buxbaum. I am a mystic, a maggid, a scholar, and an author of eleven books on Jewish spirituality. I became a religious Jew because of Martin Buber's Tales of the Hasidim, which showed me a beautiful and exalted way of life, and because of Rabbi Shlomo Carlebach, who lived that lifestyle in front of my eyes.
The mystic Jewish tradition holds a person's name to be a hint of his or her divinely ordained mission in life. My namesake, the patriarch Isaac (in Hebrew: Yitzhak), is connected with the divine attribute of Gevurah—severity or might. Yet the name itself means "he shall laugh." I understand from this that part of my task and mission in life is to turn severity into laughter. Years later I found a hasidic tale that corroborates my insight. I've translated the Hebrew:

Rebbe Baruch of Mezhibuz and Rebbe Yitzhak of Vorki.

> *Some of the disciples of Rebbe Yitzhak of Vorki asked him why, if he showed the slightest bit of anger or annoyance at someone, there were immediate repercussions--the person got ill on the spot, keeled over, and had to be carried to his sickbed where it took him a month to recover. But if Rebbe Baruch of Mezibuz (the Baal Shem Tov's overbearing grandson) was furious with someone, which was a frequent occurrence—and he actually hit people—they received a blessing! The Vorker explained to his hasidim that he himself was so gevurah-dik, as indicated by his name Yitzhak, that the slightest anger on his part produced serious consequences. But Rebbe Baruch was so hesed-dik that anyone whom he hit received a blessing as according to his name, Baruch, which means Blessed."*

Maggid Yitzchak Buxbaum told many stories. Some of them I retold in this book.

❧

YOU!

WHEREVER I GO: YOU!
WHEREVER I STAND: YOU!
JUST YOU! AGAIN YOU! ALWAYS YOU!

YOU! YOU! YOU!

WHEN IT GOES WELL WITH ME: YOU!
WHEN IT GOES WRONG WITH ME: YOU!
JUST YOU, AGAIN YOU, ALWAYS YOU!

YOU! YOU! YOU!

HEAVEN: YOU! EARTH: YOU!
UP: YOU! DOWN: YOU!
WHEREVER I TURN, AT EVERY END:
JUST YOU AGAIN! YOU! ALWAYS YOU!

YOU! YOU! YOU!

Rabbi Levi Yitzchak of Berditchev

PREFACE

This book contains a collection of Chassidic "Mayses" (i.e., short stories that are really anecdotes, parables and fable-like gems of wit and wisdom) from the Eighteenth and Nineteenth Century Chassidic Masters. Each story was carefully selected because it was either spiritually uplifting, mysteriously mystical or poignantly meaningful. These stories capture the often complex and various paths that Rebbes and their Chassidim chose to live, survive, and solve their daily struggles.

Their goal was to redeem the Divine Sparks which are hidden in all the nooks and crannies of daily existence in Galut (Exile). All of the Chassidic Rebbes serve HaShem (G'd) in their own unique way. Rabbi Chaim of Sanz stated that the Chassid who insists that only his own Rebbe knows the right path, will forfeit his share in this world and also in the World to Come. Some Rebbes promoted a daily regiment of study, others an ascetic lifestyle of fasting, and still others put emphasis on prayerful joy and dancing, or any combination of all three. In this book, all the Chassidic paths are visually linked through a common thread. Each story is complemented with an artistic vision that captures its essence and atmosphere.

My own path began long ago as a young girl in my father's study in Holland, where I was surrounded by art books and Martin Buber's collection of Chassidic stories. Later on, I would listen to many variations of the stories presented in this volume at Shabbat tables in Leyden, Amsterdam, Berlin, Jerusalem and Brooklyn. It was not always easy to find their original sources. The storytellers don't always remember the origins of the stories they tell. Some anecdotes are told in different versions and/or are ascribed to different Rebbes. Others change a bit—or a lot—over the course of several Shabbat meals. But to those who would claim or exclaim: "This is not the right version," I refer you to the highly recommended story about the Chozeh of Lublin: "The Old Harp," which I hope will inspire my readers to think of themselves as "strangers passing through," and to embellish their Shabbat meals with the words and wisdom of the Chassidic Masters. The title of the book refers to an anecdote told about Rabbi Naftali of Ropshitz who once visited a tiny village with an even smaller cemetery. The living—and lively—heritage of the Chassidic Masters will help us to avoid the spiritual graveyard.

Finally, Rabbi Menachem Mendel of Rymanow resented road repairs. What could possibly be wrong with road repairs? The Chassidic Master from Rymanow (a shtetl, presumably paved with broken roads or recently repaired ones), was insightful to realize that when people traveled on new, smooth and fast roads, they hurried along on their way—with no time at all to stop and share stories. (See: "No Peace, No Quiet"). With the profoundly inspiring messages waiting to be discovered on these pages (roadmaps), let us interrupt our hectic lives, slow down and absorb the spiritual wealth and enduring wisdom of our early Chassidic Rebbes.

A note to the reader about the layout and structure of the text: The text consists of seemingly random intermittent empty spaces and lines, interwoven short sentences, and various visual effects. It was deliberately designed this way to be faithful to the original intent, purpose and voice of the original oral narratives. The illustrations contained in this book were created over a period of twenty-five years. Some were designed specifically with this book in mind, while others were created for other Chassidic themes. I consider my art to be an inseparable part of, and in fact—the highest level of representation and expression—of my very own and very personal Yiddishkeit.

A special word of thanks to my husband, Avrom Miller, for his helpful suggestions and proof-reading the manuscript.

Shoshannah Brombacher, Flatbush (Brooklyn) 5779/2019

TABLE OF CONTENTS

INTRODUCTION

A Few Words About Chassidism

The Jewish religious climate in seventeenth and eighteenth century in Poland, Lithuania, and the Ukraine was dominated by rigorous, scholarly study of the Talmud in prestigious Talmud Academies, called Yeshivot.[1] This posed major barriers to poor, working people and the uneducated masses, who often had neither the mind-set nor the means to pursue a full-time, extended, and complicated education. The Jewish world was still recovering from the shock of the rise and fall of the self-proclaimed false messiah, Shabtai Zvi, around the year 1666, who had caused major schisms in Eastern European Jewish communities by announcing the Messianic Era and urging Jews to sell everything they owned and return to Zion. Therefore, the study of mysticism and Kabbalah, favored by Shabtai Zvi, was looked upon with suspicion by many rabbinic authorities and remained reserved for a select audience. Gemara (Talmud) and Halakhah (Jewish Law), on the other hand, were considered of major importance for every Jew. In reaction to the demands of the strict Talmud-oriented establishment, a new movement started in the eighteenth century in Ukraine and Poland, which contained mystical elements but had nothing to do with the false Messiah. Its name, Chassidism, is derived from the word Chassid, a pious (in Yiddish: frum) person, and it appealed mainly to the poor masses, which were excluded from an extended Yeshivah education.

The political situation in Eastern Europe was unfavorable for the Jews. The heinous pogroms and massacres by Chmielnicki's Cossacks in 1648 and their aftermath had left many communities decimated and uprooted, creating major social problems. Antisemitism was rampant. In fact, this was one of the reasons for Shabtai Zvi's success. Anybody who offered a glimmer of hope and redemption in such dark times was welcomed with open arms. After the massacres, groups of Jewish so-called "Holy Beggars," consisting of pious men and so-called "Hidden Tzaddikim," righteous and just people who were concealing their true, lofty nature in order to do good deeds anonymously, thus, saving the world, traveled through the countryside, attempting to reestablish, repair, educate, and support those broken communities. They offered new hope sprouting from the ashes of despair. These Holy Beggars are considered the forerunners of the Chassidim, because they initiated many of the fundamental principles and practices of Chassidism.

The founder of Chassidism, **Rabbi Israel ben Eliezer**, was born in 1698 to a poor and not very educated family in Ukraine. Orphaned at an early age, he was supported by the Jewish community, and worked various menial jobs as a shepherd and a teacher's helper, as is mentioned in the stories

---

[1] See the glossary at the end of this book for names and technical terms.

Doubt and *Sheep*.[2] Israel was an autodidact with an inclination towards mysticism, who studied at night with the biblical prophet Achia of Shilo. As a young man, Israel often withdrew into the Carpathian Mountains to meditate in solitude and study Kabbalah in secret. Later, he joined a group called Holy Beggars and explored large parts of Poland and Lithuania. One of his main practices was to give a person "bread," in the sense of improving his economic situation and removing the barrier of physical starvation which prevented him from pursuing spiritual nourishment. Only after the person was satisfied physically with "bread"—and, thus, more receptive to spiritual teachings—Israel would talk to him about HaShem (G'd) and keeping mitzvoth. When Rabbi Israel was thirty-six years old, he revealed himself as a mystical leader and a miracle worker who could even summon demons, as is illustrated in the story *The Signs*. This number of thirty-six was no coincidence. It refers to the traditional thirty-six Hidden Saints, in Yiddish called Lamed Wowniks (Thirty-Sixers), thirty-six special people in every generation who take the task upon themselves to sustain the world. Rabbi Israel acquired the honorable title **Baal Shem Tov**, the "**Master of the Good Name**," because he was able to use kabbalistic Divine Names to work miracles. He attracted a crowd of devoted and loyal students and followers, many of whom became leading Rebbes, leaders of a group Chassidim, themselves. The earliest Chassidim all belonged to the circle of the Baal Shem Tov, but after the third generation, different dynasties were formed. Usually, a son or son-in-law and occasionally a favorite student succeeded his father (in-law) or Rebbe. Some dynasties merged, like those of Karlin-Stolin. Chassidic dynasties each developed their own style with their own group-characteristics and principles, such as a propensity for asceticism or ecstasy, joy, prayer, humility, or tzedakah (see the chapter *Biographical Notes* at the end of this book).

By the time of Rabbi Israel ben Eliezer's passing in 1740, the growing Chassidic movement had many Masters, Rebbes with their own following, and was developing into a major influence throughout Jewish Eastern Europe. This came to an abrupt end through World War II, when those few Chassidim who miraculously escaped murder and the annihilation of their communities resettled in Antwerp (Belgium), Israel, and the USA, where they established important Chassidic centers.

Rebbes and their Chassidim are named by the name of their shtetl, the Eastern European town with a sizable Jewish community were their main Court is established. Often, the family name of the Rebbe is omitted. For example, Rebbe Naftali-Zvi Horowitz of Ropshitz is called R. Naftali of Ropshitz, or the Ropshitzer (Rebbe). His followers are called Ropshitzer Chassidim. Rabbi Israel, the Baal Shem Tov, is an exception; he is not known as the Medzhybizher but as the Master of the Good Name or, in short, the Besht, an acronym of Baal Shem Tov. Contemporary Chassidic groups in the USA and Israel still carry the names of the original Eastern European towns of their founders, such as the Lubavitcher Chassidim (from Lubavitch, Russia) in Crown Heights in Brooklyn, New York, or the Satmar(er) (from Satmar, Hungary) in Williamsburg in Brooklyn, New York.

---

[2] The stories in the table of contents at the beginning of this book are listed in the alphabetical order of the shtetls— towns—the rabbis are named after. For example, stories about the Besht are found under Medzhybizh and stories about Rabbi Naftali of Ropshitz under Ropshitz.

Early Chassidism attracted mainly the poor, uneducated masses in Poland, Lithuania and Russia. These felt excluded and looked down upon by the scholarly elite, which was represented by Rabbi Eliahu ben Shlomo Zalman of Vilna (1720-1779), the famous Vilna Gaon. Although most Chassidic Rebbes were themselves far from being uneducated and Talmud study is considered important in Chassidism, just like in mainstream Judaism, learning Gemara is not considered the *only* and *most important* path for the common Chassid. He must follow his Rebbe and be a meaningful and contributing member within his community to lead a spiritually fulfilling life in ways that are compatible with his abilities. Thus, Chassidism offered hope to those unable to study long hours or comprehend difficult Talmudic problems. But initially, Chassidim experienced many controversies and conflicts with the Jewish establishment. The religious, Lithuanian-style opponents of the Chassidim were therefore called **mitnaggedim** (adversaries). They play a prominent role in Chassidic anecdotes. After a Russian code of 1804 granted the hitherto considered sectarian Chassidic synagogues equal status to Litvak (Lithuanian-style) traditional, mainstream synagogues, the power of the Jewish elite establishment to ban Chassidism was diminished. The movement became gradually accepted as mainstream. In some communities Chassidim comprised the majority.

Chassidim had—and still have—several rules and customs that set them apart from Lithuanian-style Judaism, such as their own specific shechitah, the ritual slaughter of animals. Chassidic prayer distinguishes itself in many ways from the general Ashkenazy-Lithuanian rite. Chassidim abandoned the nusach ashkenaz (Ashkenazy rite) in favor of the kabbalistic rite of Rabbi Yitzchak ben Shlomo Luria of Tzfat, the Ari or Holy Lion (1534-1574), which they adapted and changed slightly for their own siddur (prayerbook). This caused anger and irritation in circles of mainstream Litvak Jews. It occasionally led to violent clashes between Chassidim and mitnaggedim. The latter tried to banish Chassidism at numerous occasions, denouncing it as sectarian or, even worse, heretic. There were several attempts to put Chassidic Rebbes and their followers in cherem, social and religious expulsion and exclusion from the Jewish Community at large. Many Lithuanian rabbis forbade their communities to eat and socialize with Chassidim or intermarry with them. They had Chassidic Rebbes imprisoned by the secular authorities on false accusations, which shows how extremely deep-rooted their dislike of Chassidism was. Several Chassidic Masters tried—in vain—to reconcile with mainstream rabbinic leaders. Some went to see the Vilna Gaon personally, whereas others set up communities in Eretz Israel to remove themselves and their followers from strife. But despite these efforts, relations between Chassidim and Litvaks remained strained. A few stories in this book, like *The Stick*, describe how students from a non-Chassidic background became attracted to the learning and lifestyle of a Rebbe and the hostile respons of their non-Chassidic environment.

A central principle in Chassidic philosophy is the important role of the **Tzaddik**, or **Rebbe**, the spiritual leader, who is endowed with mystical powers and usually has a charismatic personality. A Rebbe is not necessarily an ordained rabbi, although in practice the two nearly always overlap. His followers call themselves his Chassidim. The term Chassid ("a pious person") implements "one who has trust and faith" in HaShem and his Rebbe, his Tzaddik ("a just and righteous person"). Chassidim depend on their Rebbe in every aspect of life. They will not consider anything important, be it a religious, financial, related to family or any other matter, without first obtaining advice and approval from their Rebbe. If they can't live in his proximity they travel to visit him, for as many Jewish holidays as possible, even at great difficulties and expenses, often leaving their families and their livelihoods behind. Not all Rebbes or Tzaddikim remained in the same town where they initially set up their Court, like the Maggid of Mezritch, who never moved. Some, like the Besht, traveled around with their followers, while others were forced to move due to external circumstances. A Tzaddik's house is called his Court, which is always open to his followers and visitors. A Rebbe is assisted by a gabbay, a secretary, who accompanies him and manages appointments for Chassidim and other people who come to see ("visit") the Rebbe. The gabbay hands the Rebbe the kvitl (plural: kvitlach), the customary Chassid's note with a written request. It is usually accompanied by tzedakah (charity) money for the Rebbe, which he uses to maintain his Court and to support and feed visitors and the needy in his community. Due to the political situation in Eastern Europe, many Jews, especially among the Chassidim and including many Rebbes, were in financial straits, as is illustrated by the story *A Coin* about Rabbi Menachem Mendel of Rymanow. Therefore, mutual financial aid and physical support played an important role in the movement.

The spiritual role of the Rebbe/Tzaddik goes beyond being a religious, communal, and personal authority. The Rebbe has a tish (Yiddish for "table") in his Court, where he invites his Chassidim for special meals on Shabbat and Yom Tov, to encourage them with words of Torah and Chassidut. At the tish, an enormous amount of food is offered to the Rebbe. Whatever he doesn't eat and leaves on the table is called shirayim (leftovers), which have mystical powers. Therefore, every Chassid at the generally large table(s) wants to obtain a piece. The Rebbe is for his Chassidim an intermediary with the Higher World. He connects the Divine with the mundane. His level of understanding and prayer cannot be equalled by his followers. He collects all the prayers which could not ascend, for lack of enthusiasm of the praying person, a basic level of perfection, or sincerity, and bundles them together with his own powerful prayers, often after the non-enthusiastic or not very sincere Jews who uttered them mended their ways and did teshuvah, repentance. Thus, prayers are not lost but merely delayed. The Rebbe enables his Chassidim to live and pray with kavanah (utter devotion). He cleaves to G'd in a specific communion, called devekut (cleaving to HaShem), which is obtained through different paths, like prayer, performing specific mitzvoth, meditation, singing and dancing, or other methods.

Chassidism is a panentheistic philosophy. G'd is omnipresent, He is in everything, He is everything. G'd is even present in the mundane and must be served through corporeality (gashmiyut), through seemingly unholy or profane acts. Nothing is considered (too) insignificant. But only a Tzaddik, or Rebbe, recognizes the point where the secular is transformed into something holy. The average Chassid is unable to do this. He needs help to be lifted up, he reaches out and clings to his Tzaddik. In order to transform sinful or profane thoughts or acts into something good and holy and to elevate his Chassidim to a higher level, the Tzaddik needs to descend from his own elevated level to the lower place where his Chassidim are. Chassidim and Tzaddikim strongly depend on each other, as we see in the story Letters and Vowels about the Rizhiner Rebbe. A Tzaddik doesn't function well without his Chassidim and they cannot function without their Tzaddik. Even after a Rebbe passed away without having or naming a successor, like the Breslover Rebbe, his Chassidim continue studying his writings until this very day and visit his grave in Uman (Ukraine) to pray there.

A high spiritual level is obtained by rendering oneself "nothing," (efes), deflating one's ego to create space for the Divine, annulling oneself (bittul yesh), and living in utter humility (shiflut). Chassidic Rebbes consider the whole creation a mere garment of the Divine. Because they are part of that creation, there is no real barrier between G'd and man if he diminishes his puffed up ego (see *A Beast*). In the story *A Kind Heart*, Rabbi Meir of Dzikow values humbleness much higher than the embellishment (hiddur) of a mitzvah. A humble person has no need or desire to become angry (see *Somebody Else* and *To Lose Twice*), unless it serves educational purposes, as in *To Eat Stones*. Tzaddikim usually display a friendly, welcoming, and inclusive attitude toward people who live less than perfect lives, giving them the attention, even respect, which they would have gotten nowhere else, like the criminals in the first story of this book, *To Open the Gates*. This way, Rebbes are able to draw remote people closer to HaShem. Humble Tzaddikim and their Chassidim practice ahavat yisrael (love for one's fellow Jews), no matter how unlearned and uncouth these fellows may be. Every Jew contains a Divine spark, known as dos pintele Yid, the Jewish core, that small and sometimes hidden, dormant, ingrained piece of soul that connects all Jews. No spark must be rejected; it must rather be redeemed. This idea and many other Chassidic principles are based on kabbalistic concepts. According to the Lurianic Kabbalah of the aforementioned Ari or Holy Lion, G'd's Light filled the mystical Holy Vessels until they overflowed and broke, dispersing Holy Sparks (nitzotzot) of Divine Light into the world. These sparks became trapped everywhere and must be redeemed and reunited with their Divine Source. Therefore, the Tzaddik is persistently searching for sparks (see *The Soul of the Tzaddik* and *A Trapped Soul*). Many early Chassidim smoked tobacco in their long stemmed pipes to "release" little sparks which were trapped in the fire. Released sparks restore the mystical "Female Waters" to the Shekhinah (Divine Immanence, presented as female), which ultimately enables her to be reunited with her Divine Source, thus attributing to the Oneness of HaShem. Until now, the Shekhinah has been accompanying the Jewish people in their Exile (galut) after the Temple of Jerusalem was destroyed, in 70 CE. She mourns with the Jews and pines for the Redemption in Messianic times, (see *Galut* and *Two Roads*), and assists the Tzaddik.

Being human, Chassidim and Tzaddikim alike fall victim to temptations. Confronting evil is a dangerous—but not always avoidable—test, but the Tzaddik is better equipped for such tests than the average Chassid who, therefore, turns to his Rebbe, who can to perform miracles, possesses kabbalistic knowledge, and in some cases is able to use Divine Names to ward off demons and mortal enemies (see *The Gartel*).

Prayer is a ladder to gain devekut, communion with the Divine Source, and come closer to G'd (see Between Heaven and Earth). Joy (simchah), ecstasy, burning enthusiasm (hitlahavut), singing, jumping, and dancing are extremely important in Chassidic prayer. They gave Chassidic shuls and shtiblakh, small Chassidic prayer houses, a chaotic, even ridiculous impression in the eyes of the solemn Lithuanian establishment. Melancholy is considered a sin, because it separates a person from G'd. However, sadness with a legitimate cause is not considered a sin but rather a handicap. One should strive to be perpetually full of joy in recognizance of all the goodness that G'd benevolently provides for His creation in general, and for His Jewish people in particular. Therefore, music is held in high esteem (see *The Singing of the Angels*). Chassidim value particularly the niggun, a hummed melody without words, which is sometimes sung with supporting easy syllables like ba-ba-bam and the like. Some Rebbes use the word du, which in Yiddish means "You" and in the context of a niggun refers to HaShem (see You at the beginning of this book): du-du-du. In Yiddish such a niggun is called lovingly a dudeleh, a du-song. The Tzaddik creates and hums his niggun to help his Chassidim meditate and lift their hearts toward HaShem. Some niggunim were derived from popular gentile ditties and "liberated," as in the story *Niggun*.

This book, For Strangers Passing Through, presents a personal selection by the author, based on old and modern, written and oral sources. Some of the older, original Chassidic sources are mentioned in the chapter Biographical Notes, and modern editions in Sources and Literature. It contains a list of works on Chassidism for further reading, because many aspects of Chassidism were not mentioned in this short introduction.

All different groups of Chassidim love to share inspiring stories and anecdotes about their Rebbes. These are a valuable source of information about the early Tzaddikim (see *Pure and Holy* and *He heard what he needed*). Generally, Rebbes wrote homilies and scholarly works about Halakhah, Torah exegesis, or Kabbalistic wisdom, but no (auto-)biographies. In some cases, their writings were lost in wars or fires, therefore, the stories and anecdotes keep these Rebbes alive. Stories about Rebbes and their Chassidim were—and are—told over and over again. This is the reason that we often have more than one version. Nowadays, there are many books with Chassidic stories available, like the old *Shivchei haBesht* (published in 1805, sixty years after the Besht passed away) and the modern *Light and Fire of the Baal Shem Tov* by Yitzhak Buxbaum (2005), or the well-known collections of Martin Buber.

One of the best ways to connect to the Masters is to listen to their stories.

They speak for themselves.

FOR
STRANGERS
PASS-   ING
THROUGH

TO OPEN THE GATES

It once happened that a pious Chassid entered the synagogue and was flabbergasted to see the minyan his Rebbe had assembled to pray on behalf of a very sick man.

The Chassid was noticeably upset, because the "congregants" included: ruffians, burglars, thieves, crooks, and similar types with questionable backgrounds and ill repute! In other words, what he saw was a bunch of no-goodniks which he hoped never to come across in a dark alley, or for that matter, not even on a well lit street or in the market place.

The Rebbe, sensing his Chassid's horror,
placed a comforting hand on his shoulder, patted his back,
and patiently explained:

"Yiddel, please don't you worry!
Having such people around here is not such a bad idea.
It's not really a problem at all. Quite the opposite!

There are times when simple prayer is not enough . . .
and we need to pry open the Gates of Heaven!
At such times, we need help from the experts!

Look! Here stands Yankel the burglar and there sits Itzik One-Eye.
He claims he can open any vault with a piece of wire.
And here is Hersh the Horse; he is so strong
that he can carry away that vault on one shoulder
and can smash any lock. With such a talented and distinguished minyan praying
for that sick man, The Gates of Heaven will surely be o—p—e—n—e—d!

RABBI CHANOCH OF ALEXANDER

NOTHING

The Rebbe of Alexander declared the following:

"As long as Amalek's oppression continues,
we will remain unaware that we are nothing.
But when Amalek's reign is interrupted
we will know that we are nothing.

This is the reason: while we are oppressed,
we have no time to think.
We are too busy worrying
and focused on our enemies, doing our best
To ward off their evil schemes."

RABBI ZUSHA OF ANIPOL

A COLD SUKKAH

Zusha was an extremely poor and pious man.
Despite his frail health and lack of money,
he managed to visit many of the great Rebbes.

One time he spent Sukkoth with Rabbi David of Ostrog.
Zusha was invited to sleep
in Rabbi David's personal sukkah.
It was crowded and there were not nearly enough blankets and beds,
so he was offered a spot on the floor with the other poor folks.

Shaking from the cold, Zusha was awakened in the middle of the night
and moaned that he was freezing!
Immediately, the Prince of Fire appeared.
The sukkah soon grew so warm, that Zusha's host, Rabbi David,
pushed away the blankets from his own body, while continuing to sleep comfortably
and uninterruptedly.
When Zusha mumbled that he was no longer cold,
the Prince of Fire disappeared from the sukkah.
By morning, it was Rabbi David's turn to wake up.
But without his warm blankets, he was literally freezing.

This same strange phenomenon repeated itself night after night.
Zusha would wake up from the cold,
the sukkah would suddenly become overly warm,
the Ostroger Rebbe would wake up towards morning shaking from the cold,
because he himself would have removed the blankets during his sleep,
while the sukkah was overly warm.
When the Ostroger finally understood and realized what was happening,
he was struck with awe.
From that time on, he most respectfully addressed Zusha: "Reb Zusha."

RABBI ZUSHA OF ANIPOL

A CLOUD

Reb Zusha was very poor.
But as if that wasn't difficult enough,
he also suffered from ill health.
He could not walk too well, but always seemed content and never com-
plained.
He proclaimed that whatever came to him from HaShem was good.

When Sukkoth was over, Zusha prepared to leave Ostrog.
With a sigh, he looked at his sore feet
and the torn, dirty rags he had had wrapped around them.

OY,
    DID
THOSE
    FEET
HURT
    HIM!!!

Immediately, a cloud descended, like a pillow,
and lifted Reb Zusha up.

The Ostroger Rebbe saw it happen
and became very frightened.
He quickly offered Zusha his own horse and comfortable wagon,
if only the disturbing appearance of that cloud would disappear.

From then on, he called Zusha: "Rebbe Reb Zusha."

RABBI ZUSHA OF ANIPOL

THE BIG HAND

Some Chassidim asked Reb Zusha to explain the following verses to them:

And Israel saw Egypt dead upon the seashore (Ex. 14:30),
And Israel saw the Big Hand (Ex. 14:31).

Why does the text say *Egypt* and not *the Egyptians?*
And why is it mentioned that Israel saw the BIG HAND only afterwards?
Didn't Israel see the HAND all the time?
Shouldn't that be mentioned first?

Reb Zusha thought about this for a long time.

Then he explained:

It was the Demon of Egypt, not the Egyptians,
who put up a veil between Israel
//((((//A/// / N //D)) ///// // / / / / /)))//////((((((/ / / /
the Heavens.

Therefore, the Jews were unable to see the BIG HAND.

The Demon of Egypt perished at the Yam Suf (Red Sea)
at the same time the Egyptians died.
Only after the death of the Demon was the veil removed.

That is when Israel was finally able to behold an unobstructed view of the

HAND.

RABBI ZUSHA OF ANIPOL

SHABBOS COATS AND SHTRAYMELS

Reb Zusha and his older brother, Rabbi Elimelech, had a problem.
Whenever they ate and sang together with the Chassidim on Shabbos, they became
enveloped in enthusiasm and holiness. But, they asked themselves: what was the true
cause of these great transports of joy? Was it Shabbos itself, or were they just carried
away by the singing, the food, the fine Shabbos clothes, the atmosphere, and the ex-
hilarating company of the other Chassidim?

They decided on a little experiment!

On a routine Tuesday, they prepared a wonderful Shabbos meal,
with everything you could wish for:
delicious food, bottles of schnapps, a Shabbos samovar for hot tea, long white candles,
a goblet of red wine, golden brown challos, and a decorative, white tablecloth.
How delicious! How nice! How splendid!
They donned their long bekishes, satin coats, and their beautiful fur shtraymels,
in honor of Shabbos.
Before sunset, they gathered with some Chassidim in the house.
The dancing was so vigorous, that the walls shook
and the room radiated like fire.
The candles glowed, the wine flowed, many words of Torah were spoken,
and a sumptuous Shabbos meal was served.
Ah! So nice! Ah! So inspiring!
The ecstatic singing of the Chassidim was so loud,
that they did not notice the hustle and bustle
of a normal weekday in the streets.

Inside the room it was just plain…Shabbos!

However, Reb Zusha and Rebbe Elimelech couldn't accept
that mere objects or songs,
even beautiful words of Torah,
had caused their burning enthusiasm for this "weekday Shabbos!"

Therefore, they decided to travel to their revered Rebbe,
the Maggid of Mezritch,
to ask his advice about their dilemma!

After pouring out their heart to their Rebbe, he smiled.
The Maggid was deeply impressed with their piety.
"Now listen to me," he said.
"What is so bad if you get into a Shabbos mood
when you wear your shtraymels and your fine coats on a weekday,
with all your delicious Shabbos dishes in front of you?
For you, all these objects are connected to Shabbos
and, therefore, they attract and herald the spirit of Shabbos.
You are—thank G'd—very receptive to their *kedushah* (holiness).
I have known both of you for quite a long time!
You are very serious about serving HaShem!
Therefore, I don't see a problem here.
You want to serve HaShem
and you also enjoy Shabbos,
which is connected with serving HaShem!

Beautiful!

I wish you a good Shabbos and many more celebrations!"

Reb Zusha and his brother Rabbi Elimelech returned home in an upbeat mood.
May we all experience Shabbos as they did,
and celebrate every meal with joyful enthusiasm.

RABBI ZUSHA OF ANIPOL

TWO ROADS

On one of his travels,
Reb Zusha came upon a road
that forked into
two
different   directions.
He hesitated.   Which was the
right direction   for him?
But then,   lo and
behold,   he saw
the   Shechinah
going
ahead
of
him.

EVERY DAY

The Ohev Yisroel (the Apter Rebbe) told his students:

Every
day,
a Jew must
consider
himself to
be standing
at Har Sinai,
ready to receive
the Torah.

Why?

Because for every person
there is a past
and a future.

But not for HaShem:

EVERY DAY
He gives
the

TORAH

RABBI SHALOM OF BELZ

TOMORROW IN JERUSALEM

The men
who were drawing
water
to bake matzah,
on the eve of Pesach,
wished each other,
l'shanah haba'ah
birushalayim
(Next year in Jerusalem.)
"Why," mused the
Belzer Rebbe, "should we
wait a whole year?
We can bake matzah,
on Erev Pesach,
with this same water
in Jerusalem.

RABBI LEVI YITZCHAK OF BERDITCHEV

GOLUS

During one of his travels, the Berditchever Rebbe stayed at the house of a tanner,
a good and pious man.
But Rabbi Levi Yitzchak couldn't bear the foul smells of the tanner's trade wafting through
all the rooms, sticking to the furniture, and even to his own clothes.
As hard as the Berditchever tried,
he could not conceal his nausea and unease.
In the evening, he decided to leave the house to daven Maariv in the Beis Midrash.
It was late, though, and everyone else had left already.
The Berditchever was all alone.

There and then a thought struck him!
This is how the Shechinah feels during her travels
through this foul, forlorn world.
She is standing outside, with her head bowed low,
in the street of the tanner!

Rabbi Levi Yitzchak closed his eyes,
screamed,
and f a i n t e d.

While he was lying unconscious on the wooden floor,
the Shechinah appeared to him in a dazzling flash of light.

In a dazzling display of twenty-four beautifully colored lights,
The Shechinah looked down at him
with compassion and
encouragement.

**"Be strong, my son! You will meet terrible disasters on your path,
but don't be afraid! I will be with you!"**

RABBI LEVI YITZCHAK OF BERDITCHEV

KNEADING THE DOUGH

Perl, the rebbetzin of the Berditchever,
was an extremely pious woman.
She was once overheard saying:

"I wish that my husband
have the same holy thoughts
when he makes the blessing
over the challos
on Shabbos,
that

I

have

when

I

knead

the

dough

to

make

them."

RABBI LEVI YITZCHAK OF BERDITCHEV

WINGS TO THE CEILING

Said the Berditchever,

"The forehead of a Jew is like the Holy of Holies
of the Beis haMikdash (Temple), where the Holy Ark was kept.

If you have foul thoughts,
it is as if you bring
an idol into the Temple.

But when a holy man *davens*
with enthusiasm,
he sees the Keruvim on the Ark,
and
their
wings
are
touch-
ing
the
ceil-
ing."

RABBI LEVI YITZCHAK OF BERDITCHEV

THE SHOFAR FOR A CHOSON

When it was announced
that the Berditchever was
looking for someone to
blow the shofar for him
on Rosh haShanah,
learned and pious
people stepped
forward, all
hoping they
would be
granted
this
unique honor.

The Berditchever sent them all away.
And whom did he choose?
A plain, simple, poor, unremarkable man.

The Berditchever explained his unusual choice as follows:
"When this candidate came for the job, he mentioned to Rabbi Levi Yitzchak that he
badly needed money to find a choson for his daughter, make a wedding, and help her
set up a household.
And if he, her father, would fulfill HaShem's mitzvah to blow the shofar,
then HaShem would certainly have mercy by rewarding him with a fine son-in-law,
and enough money for a *kovedike* (dignified) wedding.
Said the Berditchever:

"The intentions
of this simple
father will
lift up all our prayers.
He is the best candidate for the task."

RABBI LEVI YITZCHAK OF BERDITCHEV

NO FIRST PAGE

The Berditchever explained
why any given volume of
the Gemara begins with
daf (leaf, folio) 2.
There simply is
no *daf* 1. It
doesn't
exist.

And why not?

This way, nobody is able to boast,
or even claim, that he studied
a large part of Gemara,
because he hasn't
even begun or
completed
the first
page.

RABBI NACHUM OF CHERNOBYL

THINGS

Once upon a time, Rabbi Nachum and his son-in-law,
Rabbi Shalom, were traveling.
Night began to fall.
So, they stopped at a village inn.
The wife of the innkeeper was about to give birth
but her labor didn't progress well.
The villagers feared for her life.
They begged the visiting rabbis for help.
They hoped the rabbis were miracle workers,
who could give them amulets
or say specific beneficial prayers.
Rabbi Nachum agreed to do his best,
if they could provide him
with a mikvah, a brand-new table, hundred and sixty copper coins,
and an empty house, where he would not be disturbed.

Rabbi Shalom, though, was surprised and disappointed.
He refused to participate in this "intrigue of superstition and magic."
Therefore, he promptly left the inn.

Later, Rabbi Shalom explained to his father-in-law
why he had refused to take part in the ritual.
He refused to depend
on the availability
of "things," objects, in order to help people.
He, Shalom, put his trust solely in HaShem!
What would happen, if he landed in a situation
where he would be unable to obtain the requisite objects?
In that case, he would be unable to provide any help!
On the other hand, his trust in HaShem was always at hand!

Rabbi Shalom stuck to this principle for the rest of his life.

RABBI MEIR OF DZIKOW

A KIND HEART

Once,
the
Rebbe
of Dzikow told a Chassid,

"On Sukkoth, all you need is a

kind heart, a humble and honest mind,

and a desire to strive for perfection.

That is absolutely much more important

than obtaining a costly, beautiful esrog,

exquisite, long willow twigs,

or nice, full hadassim,

and a flawless

lulav.

"

RABBI YITZCHAK MEIR OF GER

THE KISS

Rabbi Yitzchak Meir Alter was a student of Rabbi Moshe,
the son of the Koznitzer Maggid.

Once, Rabbi
Moshe was so pleased with
an explanation offered by his student,
that he kissed Yitzchak Meir on the forehead.
Soon thereafter, Rabbi Yitzchak Meir left Koznitz.
He felt that he was not understood correctly in
Koznitz!
What he yearned for was a teacher
who
would   rip the
flesh
off
his
bones.
Not a
teacher who
kissed
him.
After many years,
Yitzchak Meir became
the Rebbe of
Ger.

RABBI YITZCHAK MEIR OF GER

A LIFE IN DANGER

The Gerer Rebbe and the Rabbi of Pilz were
                          traveling in a wagon
          which was drawn by a couple of horses.
    When they came upon a very
                    narrow
                        road
                              in the mountains,
      along   a
              deep
                  abyss,
the horses
        neighed
              and
                  pranced,
                        coming
                  dangerously
              close
          to the
              edge!

    The Rabbi of Pilz was scared and screamed.
    But the Gerer Rebbe remained unshaken.

"Shouldn't we *always* feel as if we are in mortal danger,"
              he said,
        "didn't King David compose
          his *best* Psalms
    in the most dangerous circumstances,
          because he
      truly understood that?"

RABBI YITZCHAK ITZIK OF KALEV

NIGGUN

In Kalev, a town in Hungary, lived a little boy named Yitzchak Itzik, who had just lost his father. His widowed mother was destitute and unable to pay for her son's education. Feeling sorry for her, the community allowed her young son to take care of their sheep and geese. This way, he earned a few coins for his mother.

Meanwhile, far away from Kalev, the itinerant tzaddik Loeb ben Sarah heard
a *bas kol*, a Divine Voice, which ordered him to prepare his wagon to locate
and liberate a "trapped soul."
But where? And how?
The Voice remained silent about that.

The Tzaddik drove around for a long time.
He passed many towns in many countries.
In the end, he reached Hungary. He stopped his horse to take a break,
all the time wondering where he was.

Suddenly, Loeb ben Sarah heard a sweet, young voice
singing in Yiddish between the trees. He sensed that he was close to fulfilling
his mission. He searched, and searched, and found a little boy in tattered clothes
sitting on the mossy ground, surrounded by a flock of geese.
The little goose-herd was singing a song in his clear, young voice:

Shechinah, Shechinah, how far you are!
Golus, Golus, how long you are!
Ach, if only the Shechinah were not so far away,
Then the Golus wouldn't have to be so long!
Who will lead me out of Golus,
And reunite me with the Shechinah?

Loeb ben Sarah asked the boy, why wasn't he in cheder (school), and where had he learned that beautiful song?

"My mother has no money for cheder," said the little goose-boy, "and I learned this melody from the other shepherds in the woods."

"I noticed them on my way, but they are not Jewish," protested the Tzaddik, "do they really sing such songs?"

"Of course not," said the boy, "I just changed the words a bit. This is their song:

> *Forest, forest, how huge you are!*
> *Rose, rose, how far you are*
> *Oh, were the forest not so huge,*
> *Then the rose wouldn't be so far!*
> *Who will lead me out of this forest,*
> *And reunite me with my rose?"*

Loeb ben Sarah realized, that this melody was a holy *niggun*. The goose-boy had liberated it from the Hungarian shepherds, for whom it was a simple Hungarian love song about their longing for their wives while they were far from home with their flocks. But the deeper meaning of this song was about the Divine Presence, the Shechinah, and Golus, the Jewish Exile.

Loeb ben Sarah asked little Yitzchak Itzik to bring him to his mother.
When he saw the dire poverty of the widow, he offered to pay for the boy's education and take care of him, which the mother gladly accepted.

Many years later, Yitzchak Itzik became known as the famous
Singing Rebbe of Kalev.

RABBI YITZCHAK ITZIK OF KALEV

SOAP

The Kalever Rebbe mused about the Shabbos song,
Ki eshmera shabbat E-l yishmereni
(*Because I keep Shabbos, HaShem will keep me safe*),
which contains the strange phrasing:
...*therefore, on Shabbos I cleanse my heart **as if** soap (khe-vorit*).

What does that mean, "***as if*** *soap?*"
You wash *with* soap
but you don't "wash" soap.
Now, the holy Shabbos—which **is** your soap—
can make your heart so clean and pure
that it is able to wash other hearts
and cleanse them,
just like soap cleanses other things.

The Chassid who told this story about the Kalever Rebbe
became a Master himself.
He claimed that the Kalever had made him a Jew, a real Jew.

How did that happen?

The Rebbe had pulled the
soul of that Chassid
out of his body.
He cleansed
and purified it
with his own
clean soul,
like soap,
and then put it back
into the body of the Chassid.

68

נשמה טהורה

RABBI YITZCHAK ITZIK OF KALEV

GUESTS

The son of the Kalever Rebbe married Rayzel, the daughter of Rabbi Zvi Hersh of Zydaczow. The young couple lived with Rayzel's parents. But for Pesach, the Kalever Rebbe, Rabbi Yitzchak Itzik, invited his son and daughter-in-law to his house in Kalev.

Rayzel wasn't happy to spend Pesach in Kalev. Many customs there were so different from those of her home town and her own family, but she went with her husband, of course.

Unlike the Seder in her parents' house, the Seder in Kalev started very late. Her father-in-law stood at the window for a long time, as if he were expecting someone. But who might that person be? All the guests had already arrived and were seated around the table.

All of a sudden, the window flew open! Rayzel saw a carriage streaming down from the sky. It landed softly in front of the house.
Three venerable men and four valorous women stepped out. They greeted the Kalever Rebbe warmly and conversed with him in hushed voices. Soon, they boarded their carriage again and took off toward the Heavens. As if nothing out of the extraordinary had just occurred, the Kalever Rebbe turned around, without an explanation returned to the table, and began the Seder.

Rayzel didn't dare ask about the carriage. But after the seder her husband explained it to her. For years, his father had been praying so fervently for redemption from Golus, Exile, that the Fathers and Mothers themselves had descended from Gan Eden. They had come to inform the Kalever Rebbe that the time for Moshiach had not arrived.

Not yet.

RABBI AHARON OF KARLIN

BETWEEN HEAVEN AND EARTH

The Karliner Rebbe explained the following verse:

Behold
   a ladder
      set on
         the
            earth,
               and
                  its
                     top
                        reach-
                           ed
                              to
                                 Heaven. [1]

If a Jew is grounded and stands firmly on the earth, his head reaches toward Heaven. In other words, he has to take care of business in this world. He must work to support his family and his community. But in the meantime, his head must concentrate on HaShem, the Torah, mitzvoth, and on helping others.

---

[1] Gen. 28:12

RABBI AHARON OF KARLIN

THE ROAD TO KARLIN

A Chassid in search of a Rebbe
               decided to travel a
                        great distance
                to Karlin.
           On the way,
      people asked him
why he couldn't find
        a Rebbe who lived closer
                to his own
                   town?
                      Aren't there
                Rebbes
          and Chassidim
      everywhere?
Answered the Chassid:
   "Because I can read everybody's thoughts."
   "If that is really true," somebody asked him,
   "can you tell me what I'm thinking of right now?"
   "You are thinking of HaShem," said the Chassid.
   "No, wrong! I am not!" answered the man.
   "Now you see," answered the Chassid,
            "That's
          why
             I
               go
                all
                the
                  way
                to
                  Karlin."

RABBI MOSHE OF KOBRYN

JOY

The Kobryner Rebbe was very poor.
He had neither money nor material wealth.

He used to say,

"If only poor people would know
how rewarding it is to be poor,
they would dance for joy!"

Being poor is never easy.
But you are, at least, not distracted or deceived
by the devious and deceitful financial schemes of opportunists
or seduced by sinful material pursuits.

A poor man is able to focus on HaShem.
A poor man has time to study Torah.

A poor man places his trust in HaShem
and not in his own skills,
talents,
cleverness,
abilities,
succes,
money,
jobs,
social positions,
or the economy.

He places his trust in HaShem.

RABBI PINCHAS OF KORETZ

THE ESROG

Shortly before the Holy Baal Shem Tov passed away,
he whispered an enigmatic message into the ear of Rabbi David of Ostrog:
"There is a bear in the forest. Pinchas is a wise man."

Rabbi David figured immediately who the "bear" was. Who else but the famous Rabbi Dov Baer of Mezritch whom the Besht held in high esteem.
But much to his surprise, he learned that the man named Pinchas was a poor, obscure teacher of young children, a simple *melamed*, who lived in the town of Koretz. Pinchas wasn't a scholar. He wasn't even a follower of the Baal Shem Tov. This Pinchas was so poor and destitute, that he didn't posses his own oven, which even the poorest people managed to have. And even if he had an oven, he never would have been able to afford the cost of firewood anyway. Therefore, the community allowed him to sleep behind the oven in the Beis Midrash to keep warm in winter.

For the longest time, Rabbi David of Ostrog used top purchase two esrogim (citrons) for the festival of Sukkoth: one was a present for the Besht, and the other one was for his own personal use. This year however, he bought three esrogim: one for himself, one for Rabbi Dov Baer, and one for the unknown and highly mysterious Pinchas of Koretz. As it turned out, Rabbi David wasn't able to make the trip all the way to faraway Koretz, and instead sent a messenger to deliver the prized esrog to Pinchas in a lavishly decorated box.

Meanwhile, back in Koretz, no-one knew a thing about the cryptic words of the Besht or Rabbi David's arrangement to deliver three esrogim.
Unfortunately, not one man in the entire Holy Community of Koretz had managed to obtain an esrog for Sukkoth that year. For one thing, even under the best of circumstances, these once-a-year fruits were rare and very expensive. But this year, there were—in addition to rising prices—unforeseeable problems with deliveries and transportation.

On the first day of Sukkoth, the entire Holy Community of Koretz began the prayer service without one single esrog. What else could they do? They completed the first part of the morning prayers. But when they arrived at the specific prayers dealing with taking the esrog

in one's hand and making the required blessing, Pinchas stood up from where he was seated next to the oven, and fervently pleaded with the Congregation to wait for an esrog.

But nobody listened to him. What's the use of waiting and fooling oneself? There just weren't any esrogim available in Koretz and they knew it! But then, for some strange reason, they hesitated. There was something compelling about Pinchas' pleas.

Did he know something that they did not know?

Well, a short while later, a gentile messenger knocked at the door of the shul.

He carried a fancy looking package with a letter. It was addressed to:

Pinchas, the Head of the Sons of the Galut

The messenger opened the package for Pinchas, who then lifted a beautiful esrog from its soft, little bed of wool in the box. The people gasped.

Pinchas then approached the Bimah and led those gathered in the synagogue on that day in the formal Succoth prayers.

All the *tefillot* (prayers) went straight up, and the beautiful esrog lifted the hearts of the Jews with its sweet fragrance.

Years later, when Rabbi Pinchas had become a most famous and celebrated Chassidic Rebbe, the Holy Community of Koretz understood the visionary foresight of the Besht.

RABBI PINCHAS OF KORETZ

OUTSIDE

After the miraculous occurrence with the esrog, Rabbi Pinchas became an overnight celebrity. Chassidim flocked to his home to study with him and be in his company, as Chassidim do when they admire their Rebbe. But Pinchas himself resented that! Those admirers left him with little or no time to pursue his hunger and thirst for concentrated study of Torah in solitude. He missed the old days when they left him alone behind the oven. Now, people besieged him night and day—non-stop—with all types of problems, questions, and matters. Rabbi Pinchas became so unbearably frustrated, that he begged HaShem to make him unpopular! He wished everybody would just leave him alone. Much to his surprise, his prayers were fulfilled. Even his poor wife had a difficult time getting support from their neighbors to put up their sukkah. Although some felt sorry for the good soul that she was, no-one was willing to spend time helping her and her husband with the construction. On Sukkoth, no one invited Rabbi Pinchas to visit, nor did anybody visit him to make a blessing in his sukkah.

On the first evening of the Festival, Rabbi Pinchas entered and sat alone in his sukkah to fulfill the mitzvah to "dwell in booths." He pronounced the prescribed blessings and chanted the invitation for the first of the seven Ushpizin, the biblical guests. He heard a sound. There was a rustle outside! At first, Rabbi Pinchas ignored it. Maybe it was just a frightened cat. But when the sound kept repeating itself, he stuck his head out of the sukkah to investigate. Lo and behold, it wasn't a cat, but Avraham Avinu himself standing right next to the opening of the sukkah with a pained look on his face. Reb Pinchas was at first taken aback, then exalted, and became excitedly eager to usher his most honored guest into the sukkah. But, the Patriarch declined. How could he, the most considerate and thoughtful host who served faraway travelers, wayfarers and angels — sit down in a sukkah that excluded other guests, neighbors, beggars — not even a cat?

Rabbi Pinchas understood the message. He prayed and begged HaShem to restore his love for people and their love for him.

Afterwards, he became the great Chassidic Master with many followers.

RABBI PINCHAS OF KORETZ

SHE DOESN'T REPEAT

Said Rabbi Pinchas,

"The soul of a man is his teacher.
There is no man, whose soul doesn't continuously teach him."

"Then why," people asked him,
"do things go wrong?"
"Why do people make wrong decisions?"
"Why don't people listen more closely to their souls?"
" Why don't they follow the wise advice of their souls?"
" Why do they miss and reject the teachings of their souls?"

Rabbi Pinchas answered thus:

"The
soul
of a
person
is
teaching
him
continuously,
but
she
doesn't
repeat
herself."

RABBI PINCHAS OF KORETZ

SINGING

Rabbi Pinchas of Koretz said:

"When a man is singing,
he can't always raise his voice
to find the right
tone or melody.

But then another man joins him,
raises his voice,
and teaches him the correct melody.

From that moment on,
the first one can raise his voice
as well.

This is the secret of a soul cleaving to a soul."

Chassidim must encourage, help, and support
each other. And their
Rebbe
encourages,
supports,
and
carries
them
all.

RABBI PINCHAS OF KORETZ

THE SOUL OF THE TZADDIK

There is a kabbalistic concept known as the "Breaking of the Vessels."
When HaShem created the world, all the Divine Vessels were filled with G'd's light,
until the enormous pressure caused them to break.

Many

rays

and

sparks

of

Divine

light

flowed

down

and

became

d i s

p   e

r   s

e

d.

Said Rabbi Pinchas,

"Also in the soul of the Tzaddik, vessels break apart!"

RABBI ISRAEL OF KOZNITZ (THE KOZNITZER MAGGID)

TO EAT STONES

The Koznitzer Maggid once asked a rich man
what he usually ate for dinner.

This rich man was very ascetic.
He led a Spartan lifestyle.
He answered, with pride,
that he ate and drank nothing more
than a few slices of hard, dark bread with salt,
and washed them down with a jug of plain water.
(Such self-sacrifice would certainly please the Rebbe, he thought)

"Fool!" scolded the Maggid,
"Go home!
Eat meat, cake, fine fish, and other delicacies!
Drink aged wine!
And if you don't follow my exact instructions,
You will be hearing from me the very same day! I know where you live!
And then, I'm not finished with you!"

Later, he explained to his students why he acted so firmly with this wealthy man.
Wasn't it this man's own business to eat what he wanted
and not eat what he not wanted?

No! It was not!

And why not?
Because, if he, such a wealthy man, could live on dry bread and salt,
he might think that poor people could live on dry stones.
And why, then, would a rich person ever help his destitute
brothers by giving **tzedakah**?

RABBI ISRAEL OF KOZNITZ (THE KOZNITZER MAGGID)

BLACK FIRE ON WHITE FIRE

Once,
the Koznitzer   Maggid lectured
in Apt on the occasion   of his father's Yohrzeit.
But when the Holy   Community   of Apt invited him
to speak again   the following   year, the Maggid refused.
He had serious doubts if   his
Dvar Torah   of the year before   had   changed the
minds and lives   of his audience for   the better.   He had observed
people snoring and snoozing,   while others
appeared totally bored. Some   even   stared at him   pretending
and feigning as if they understood his lecture.   However,   he sensed clearly they did not, nor
did they   bother to ask him   questions.
In fact, the Maggid even recalled   overhearing a heated and vociferous   conversation   going on in
the very back of the   synagogue
about a business deal that made no attempt   to even disguise itself   in hushed tones.
In short,   he preferred to spend   his energy   on a more deserving and worthy
audience   than the   Jews of Apt!   The delegation of the Holy
Community of Apt   listened, heard what they needed to hear,   apologized, and humbled themselves
with their heads   bowed low.   Later, they gathered   for a second time
near the door of the Rebbe's inn.
Then, unexpectedly,   a simple   laborer stepped   forward. He slowly
approached the Maggid: "Holy Rabbi, who says   that your last speech had no impact? It had a
great impact on me!!! When you quoted,
"I have set HaShem always before me…,"[1]
I saw
the Holy Name   **in front of me,**
written in   **black fire on**   **white fire,**
and I still see
it in front of me
now!   I see it all the time!"

That year the Koznitzer Maggid lectured in Apt.

---

[1] Ps. 16:8

RABBI ISRAEL OF KOZNITZ (THE KOZNITZER MAGGID)

THE SISTER

The Koznitzer Maggid was always involved in acts of *chesed* (kindness), helping the poor. For example, he used to buy rolls of cloth, and order a tailor to make shirts, pants, and coats for local orphans.

Whenever the cloth merchants came to his house with their supplies, he would have them wait while he disappeared to a certain room. There, he would consult with the soul of his late sister. She had passed away at a young age, but her soul was granted special permission to dwell in her brother's house in order to assist him with his charitable projects. But in addition, however, she told the Maggid everything about the servants, whom she could observe and hear. They could not see or hear her.

She knew exactly who lied,
who stole food from the pantry,
who was dishonest,
and who was lazy.

Her brother was very annoyed by her tell-tale habits, her *lashon harah*.
He requested repeatedly that she keep her mouth shut.
One time, when she failed to curb her tongue again,
he became so furious, that he screamed at her:

"WOULDN'T YOU TAKE A BREAK!?"

This was the last time
the soul of the sister
had entered the
house.

RABBI ISRAEL OF KOZNITZ (THE KOZNITZER MAGGID)

A SOLDIER'S SONG

At the time of the Koznitzer Maggid, countless young, Jewish boys suffered the misfortune of being forcibly drafted into the army of the Czar, for torturously long periods of service—even up to twenty-five years. Many of the cantonists, as these children were called, died from physical and spiritual deprivation; others were forcibly converted, may such a fate only befall our enemies.
It is clear, that none of them received a proper Jewish education.
One such young "soldier" happened to be in Koznitz with his regiment at Pesach time.
He asked permission to attend the Maggid's seder.
The Maggid warmly invited him to his table.

After the seder, the Chassidim chanted the traditional song,
peduyim le-tzion be-rinnoh...
(*redeemed to Tzion with joy…*)

When the soldier heard *peduyim*,
he shouted in Russian
мы будем, (*mbudyim, Let's go!*)

The Maggid beamed.
"Yes! *peduyim!* мы будем!
We are ready to go!"

But when the Chassidim turned around . . .
Where was the little soldier all of a sudden? He had disappeared!

RABBI ISRAEL OF KOZNITZ (THE KOZNITZER MAGGID)

THE SHALOM BAYIS KUGEL

After
a very nasty fight, a man and his wife went to the
Koznitzer Maggid for a divorce. "My wife," complained the
man, "always bakes a delicious *kugel* for Shabbos! I love that *kugel*! I
cannot resist that *kugel*! The whole week, I work, I toil, I schlep for that
kugel! When I just think about it, my mouth starts watering! But what does
that foolish woman do? After kiddush, do I get my *kugel*? Nooooo! First, she
serves gefilte fish! Then soup, then lots of potatoes! Then chicken! Then come
vegetables and compote, plums and noodles!! By that time I'm so full that I *plotz*, I
cannot possibly swallow one more bite! Then—only then—she finally decides to
bring in the *kugel*! Shouldn't I divorce her?"
And he muttered a few more words that people normally don't say in front of a rabbi.
The wife offered an explanation for her behavior: in her parents' home it was always
done this way! Therefore, she didn't and couldn't and wouldn't budge! Never!
After some thinking,
the Koznitzer Maggid offered a solution. From now on, the wife should bake two
kugels: one to serve right after kiddush, and the other one to serve after the gefilte
fish, soup, chicken, potatoes, noodles, plums, compote, and all those other delicious
but heavy, filling dishes, as was the custom in her parents' house.
The couple left, reconciled.
From then on, the Koznitzer Maggid always had two *kugels* at his Shabbos
table: one to eat after the main course and one right after kiddush. This
latter one he called the "*shalom bayis kugel*". Why? Because there is
nothing more important than *Shalom Bayis*, peace at home!
Even if it means that you have to eat
two *kugels*!

RABBI MENACHEM MENDEL OF KOTZK

A FUR-COAT

?

(—)
The
Kotzker
Rebbe referred to a
certain colleague of his
as a "tzaddik in *pels,* (with a
fur-coat)." What did he mean
by that? Don't most people
here wear fur-coats in winter?
When it's freezing outside, some
rabbis heat their big rooms with a fire.
Everybody in those rooms—friends,
students, poor people, and colleagues,
they all benefit and stay warm
and cozy. But certain rabbis put
on a warm fur-coat. And then,
the only person who stays warm
is the rabbi wearing the fur-coat.

RABBI MENACHEM MENDEL OF KOTZK

HE HEARD WHAT HE NEEDED

The Kotzker Rebbe had a strong Lithuanian background. Later, he turned to Chassidism, and after many years became a great Chassidic Master himself. When people asked him how and why that change happened, he explained it with the following story.

Once, when he was a young student on his way to the study hall,
he saw a story-teller in the street.
That was nothing special.
They were very common
and drew large crowds at the market-square
or on street corners.
Normally, he did not stop to listen to them,
because that would take precious minutes away
from his Torah study.
This time, however, he felt compelled to pause and listen.
He himself did not understand why.

Young Menachem was mesmerized
by the tales about the Baal Shem Tov and his Chassidim.
That was the moment he decided to study Chassidut.

Said the Kotzker:

"That story-teller told what he knew.
And I heard what I needed to hear."

RABBI MENACHEM MENDEL OF KOTZK

LIKE A WOLF

Said
the Kotzker,
"If you run into a
wolf,
you do not
contemplate
your fear,
think it over,
or examine
it from
all sides:

YOU

JUST

FEAR!!

That is how we must fear HaShem."

RABBI MENACHEM MENDEL OF KOTZK

THE SUFFERING HUNTER

A Jewish hunter lived all alone in a hut in the woods. He hardly observed any mitzvoth, nor did he know, study, or have any interest in Torah.

One day, Eliyahu HaNavi, may his memory be blessed, visited the hunter in the disguise of a lost traveler. When the wandering Prophet observed the hunter tasting food without making the required blessing or washing his hands, he asked him why didn't care to live as a Jew?

"How, or where," mumbled the hunter with his mouth full of bread, "could I, of all people? I know nothing! I live in the woods. I don't even know anybody around here whom I could ask about Jewish customs."

Then Eliyahu wanted to know, who had taught the hunter his hunting skills?

Where did he get his knowledge about the animals, about the forest?

Did the hunter learn and refine his talents of trapping and shooting in a short time, or even in one shot? Or, did he try and practice his skills again, and again, and over again? Did it take him a long time? And what did he do before he had fully mastered the skills of catching animals? How did he live? What did he eat?

The hunter stared at the floor in front of him, and mumbled,

"I was miserable. I suffered. I had to learn very fast,
or else I would have starved..."

Retorted the Prophet,

"And couldn't suffering teach you how to find HaShem?"

When the students of the Kotzker heard this story they didn't ask questions.
They understood.

RABBI MENACHEM MENDEL OF KOTZK

FAITH AND TRUTH

Rabbi Simchah Bunim of Pshiskhe asked
his student, Rabbi Mendel,
how he would translate the word
emunah,
which many translate as *faith.*

Said Rabbi Mendel,
"*emunah* implies both Faith and Faithfulness,
but also Truth,
because *HaShem's Word is Truth,*
ve-khol ma'asehu ve-emunah, and all His deeds are in truth," [1]

HaShem is good, His mercy is everlasting,
and His emunato (truth), endureth for all generations." [2]

Rebbe Reb Bunim was happy to have a student with such insight.

He   burst

out

in

song.

[1] Ps. 33:4

[2] Ps.100:5

RABBI MENACHEM MENDEL OF KOTZK

FEH! MONEY!

When he was a young student,
 Menachem Mendel was extremely poor.
His clothes were threadbare and in fetters.
He did not even have a decent, warm coat.
In winter, he froze and suffered constantly from the cold.

Once, Rabbi Bunim of Pshiskhe sent one
of his students to distribute a large sum of
tzedakah (charity) money among poor *bochurs* (students)
in the Beis Midrash.
Exactly at the moment that Rabbi Bunim's student
had given away the very last coin,
poor, cold, hungry Menachem Mendel entered the room.
The student of Rabbi Bunim apologized profusely,
because he had nothing left to give him.
Mendel made a face, and said, "Feh! Money!"

For
a long time
afterwards, the student
who had distributed the
Tzedakah coins couldn't
even look at money
without getting
nauseous.

RABBI CHAIM OF KROSNO

ON A ROPE

Once, Rabbi Chaim of Krosno passed the market-square and observed an acrobat doing
acrobatics
  on

   a

    rope
     high

      above

        the
         ground.

The Rebbe normally passed such street-acrobats without paying attention, because he
did not want to take away time from his Torah study. But now he stopped to watch the
spectacle with keen interest.

    He explained to his students,
   "If that man high up there would think about the money
   that he earns with his act, instead of concentrating on the rope,
     he would surely
      make

      a

      fatal

      mis-

      take

      and

      plunge

      to

      his

    d e a t h.
  Mustn't we serve HaShem the same way?"

RABBI MORDECHAI OF LECHOWITZ

A BEAST

Rabbi Mordechai of Lechowitz explained the verse,

"But   I
was   stupid,
and
had no insight,
I was as a beast with
You," [1] as follows: *"HaShem,*
I don't care to be stupid,
I don't even care to
be a beast, if only
I can be with
Y O U!"

---

[1] Ps. 73:22

RABBI DAVID OF LELOV

A BETH DIN WITH A HORSE

Once, the Lelover Rebbe was compelled to make a trip on a Friday.
He could not postpone it until after Shabbos.
While he sat in the coach, concentrating on his *sefer*,
the wheels came to a sudden

g..ri..n-..<<=…=<<din..g>>..==<<ha…l..t.

The horse, for no obvious reason, refused to move one step further.

The anxious coach-driver knew they were running out of time to get home before Shabbos!
They had to hurry! Frantically, he started to whip the animal.
But the Lelover restrained his arm.

Yes, it was Erev Shabbos, and yes, the Rebbe was in a big hurry.
Yes, the horse belonged to the driver. Yes, it was his property.
But no, the Rebbe wouldn't let him beat his dumb, poor animal,
even if that's what the man always did under similar circumstances.

And why not?

This is why. When the driver, the horse, and the Rebbe would arrive in the Next World—after hundred and twenty years—the soul of the poor horse might turn out to be a *gilgul*, a reincarnated human soul. It would force the souls of the Rebbe and the wagon driver to a heavenly Beth Din.

And how honorable would it look for them
to be entangled in a court case with a horse!?

RABBI DAVID OF LELOV

SOMEBODY ELSE

One day, Rabbi David was walking in the street, when suddenly, without any warning, a
woman attacked him from behind.
Screaming and cursing,
she beat him
and clawed him.
She hurled hurtful
words at him.
She raged like a wild, ferocious cat.

It took the bystanders a great deal of effort to pull her off the Rebbe's back. She kept fuming
while they restrained her. While her hapless victim was helped to his feet by some students,
she peered into his face. The Rebbe was confused, bruised, and covered with dirt and grime
of the street. His coat was torn, his glasses askew, and his beard was tangled.

The woman turned deadly pale. She howled:

"OY GEVALT!!!!"

She was dumbfounded. Numb. This was not the man she thought she had recognized from
behind. She mistakenly believed she had finally caught hold of her abusive husband—who
had long ago abandoned her and their young children, and shamelessly left them penniless to
fate. She burst into tears out of shame, remorse, and frustration.
Rabbi David painfully straightened his back. When he finally understood from her sobs what
had happened, he was not angry. He comforted her, saying that it wasn't him she had beaten
up, but her eloped husband.
How often doesn't this happen?
You beat someone up
because you are convinced
that he or she is
somebody else?

RABBI SHNEUR ZALMAN OF LIADI (THE ALTER REBBE)

TO LISTEN AND TO UNDERSTAND

As
a young
boy, Zalman, later
known as
the Alter Rebbe,
accompanied Rabbi Pinchas
of Koretz on his way to Mezritch.
They drove through the woods and
heard the birds singing on their branches.
Each bird sounded differently; each one had its
own melody—happy or sad, distant or close,
high or low. Rabbi Pinchas knew the
language of the birds. He offered to teach
it to the boy. But little Zalman shook his
head and declined. Many years
later, the Alter Rebbe drove
himself through the
woods and the
fields with his
young grandson.

This
time, too, the
birds were
chirping and singing,
and the forest was filled
with a concert of trills and
tweets, tremolos, hoots, and
flutes. The
Alter Rebbe listened intently.
"You hear the birds talking?" he asked his grandson, "They have long conversations in their own language. They even have their own alphabet. But to understand them is not as difficult as you may think. All you have to do is to listen carefully. And pay attention to them."

RABBI SHNEUR ZALMAN OF LIADI (THE ALTER REBBE)

THE EMPTY SEAT

As a student, young Shneur Zalman
used to join the *tish* of Rabbi Menachem of Vitebsk.
He sat himself at the far end of the table
with the other young *bochurs* (students),
because he was very humble.
The *tish* was always crowded.
With so many people around,
who took notice of the poor students at the far end?

It once happened, on Erev Rosh HaShanah,
that Shneur Zalman's seat remained empty.
Rabbi Menachem noticed this immediately.
He got up and walked outside, looking for the missing student.

Finally, he found him in the deserted Beis Midrash.
Rabbi Menachem glanced at him
and returned to the table.

"Do not disturb him,"
said Rabbi Menachem.

"He is happy with HaShem,
and HaShem is happy with him."

RABBI SHNEUR ZALMAN OF LIADI (THE ALTER REBBE)

THE RETURN

After the passing of the Maggid of Mezritch,
the Alter Rebbe decided to leave that town.

Rabbi Avraham the Angel, the son of the Maggid,
gave him a personal send off and sat next to him in the wagon.

Said the Angel:
"Start the horses,
and let them run—until they forget that they are horses!"

Said Rabbi Zalman Shneur:

"To master *this* path in the service of HaShem will take a while!"

He turned the
      wagon
         around
            and went
      straight back
to Mezritch.

RABBI YAAKOV YITZCHAK OF LUBLIN (THE SEER OF LUBLIN)

A SIMPLE COACH-DRIVER

A simple, unremarkable, and uneducated coach-driver asked some Chassidim of the Seer to deliver his *kvitl* (a note addressed to a Rebbe) for him to the Chozeh of Lublin.

The piece of paper contained a request to remember the coach-driver's name and give him a blessing. The Chozeh read it, and exclaimed:

> ***"The name of this man lights up!***
> ***At this same moment his soul radiates pure light!"***

The puzzled Chassidim were curious. They wanted to know who that seemingly simpleton coach-driver really was. They searched for him, and finally found him in a house where people were celebrating the wedding of two poor orphans. An hour earlier, the coach-driver drove past that house and stopped his horse after hearing music. Although he was neither invited, nor even remotely familiar with anyone at the wedding celebration, he decided right there and then to join the party. The coach-driver sang and danced, with such vigor and enthusiasm, that he made everybody around him just plain happy!

But when it came time for the bride to present her choson with the traditional wedding gift of a tallis, it turned out that she had neither the tallis nor money to buy one. Oy gevalt! There was no tallis! A quarrel broke out between several guests and relatives. The whole wedding was nearly canceled! The coach-driver felt sorry for the innocent and embarrassed young orphans. He took out all his hard-earned money—and behold, it was just enough to buy a fine, white tallis.

This simple coach-driver saved the day and the wedding and by so doing, rescued a "House of Israel".

And his name shone forth like a flash of light!

RABBI YAAKOV YITZCHAK OF LUBLIN (THE SEER OF LUBLIN)

TO LOSE TWICE

One day, the Chozeh of Lublin asked his
rebbetzin to serve him his supper earlier
than usual. He wanted to leave
the house in timely fashion,
to do an act of *chesed*.

However, on that same day, some things were out of
order in the kitchen. The food could
not be served to the Seer earlier, as
requested. In fact, quite the
opposite, it was served much
later than usual.
Did the Seer become angry?

No.

He figured, that he had already suffered one
loss, because he would be late for his
mitzvah. Should he suffer a second
loss by losing his temper
as well?

RABBI YAAKOV YITZCHAK OF LUBLIN (THE SEER OF LUBLIN)

THE OLD HARP

A Chassid noticed that the Chozeh used to take a pinch of tobacco while he davened. This irritated him tremendously. He found it utterly disrespectful. Although the Chassid did not dare to tell that to his Rebbe's face, the Lubliner sensed it anyway. He decided not to shame the Chassid, but to teach him and his fellow students a lesson with a story.

Once, a king stood near a window in his palace. He heard a harp playing in the street beyond the garden wall. The melody was so sweet. It was music to the king's ears! He summoned his servants to find the street-musician and bring him into the palace. They came back with an old man with an old harp tucked under his arm. From that day on, the old man played his sweet and undulating tunes in the big hall of the palace. How the king loved his melodies! They made him calm and happy, peace flowed into his heart. But one thing annoyed the king greatly: the old man frequently interrupted his music to tune his old, rickety harp, which had seen better days.

The king offered the harp player a brand new instrument from his royal music room, but the old man would not have it. He explained, "Your Majesty, for sure my Lord the King has his own beautiful orchestra, with brand new expensive instruments, that are played by the most talented musicians in this country, who attended the best conservatories here and abroad. But if it pleases my Lord, the King to listen to the tunes of an old man, his Majesty will have to put up with the limitations and peculiarities of my art and my tools."

The Chassid
////// of the
//////// Lubliner
//////// heard the
////// story and
he understood.

RABBI YAAKOV YITZCHAK OF LUBLIN (THE SEER OF LUBLIN)

MANY PATHS

Rabbi Baer, the Radoshitzer Rebbe,
once asked the Seer about the right path to serve HaShem.

Answered the Seer:

"There is no such thing as *the* right path to serve HaShem.

There is a path of learning;
      there is a path of fasting;
there is a path of feasting;
      there is a path of meditating;
there is a path of dancing;
      there is a path of studying;
there is a path of singing, etc…
etc…
        etc…
etc…
        etc…
etc…

There are many, many, many, many different paths!

No two people are the same.
We each have our own appropriate path.

But the path that *you* choose,
that path you must follow with all your might."

RABBI ISRAEL BEN ELIEZER OF MEDZHYBIZH (THE BAAL SHEM TOV)

DOUBT

Israel ben Eliezer lost his parents at an early age.
The young orphan had no money to support himself.
The community felt sorry for him,
and gave him a job as a teacher's helper.
But Israel often left the classroom
and disappeared into the woods, to be alone and meditate.

People doubted that he would ever grow up to be a decent Jew,
let alone an educated Jew.

But what did they know?

Israel's time to reveal himself had not yet come.

RABBI ISRAEL BEN ELIEZER OF MEDZHYBIZH (THE BAAL SHEM TOV)

THE GARTEL

At night, the prophet Achia of Silo used to visit young Israel ben Eliezer to teach him Torah. One time, Israel used the Heavenly knowledge he had learned to cross the River Dniester. He threw his *gartel* (prayer belt) onto the water, uttered a secret, and mystical Holy Name, and crossed the stream to the other side by standing on his gartel. This way, he stayed dry, and saved a lot of time by not having to search for a ford, bridge, or boat. But all his life, he felt deep remorse for having used a Holy Name just for his own convenience.

Years later, when Rabbi Israel was a great and famous scholar, people called him the Baal Shem Tov, the "Master of the Good Name." They knew that he possessed knowledge and skills that allowed him to use secret and mystical Holy Names.

Once again, the Baal Shem Tov found himself standing in front of a river.
But this time, he had to run for his life with anti-semitic thugs on his heels, threatening to maim and kill him.

> A second time,
>
> he threw his belt on the
>
> water, and crossed safely
>
> to the other
>
> side of the
>
> river. But
>
> he didn't
>
> use a Holy Name.
>
> He used only his
>
> trust in
>
> HaShem.
>
> And that
>
> was
>
> enough.

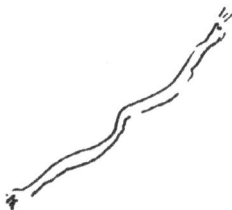

RABBI ISRAEL BEN ELIEZER OF MEDZHYBIZH (THE BAAL SHEM TOV)

SHEEP

It once
came to pass,
the Besht was in the
mountains, far
away from people,
houses, huts, and villages. He was
forced to spend Shabbos
in nature. Since there was
no shul around, he davened
in a field. The sheep grazing
nearby saw him and stopped
eating. They stood on their
hind-legs until the Besht had
finished his prayers. Why
did they do that?
The   *kavanah*,
or   inten-
tion,   of
the   Baal
Shem   Tov
was
so strong, that every creature around him was compelled
to resume its original position,
just as it once had been standing near the Throne of HaShem.

RABBI ISRAEL BEN ELIEZER OF MEDZHYBIZH (THE BAAL SHEM TOV)

HIM ALONE

Many evenings,
Rabbi Israel Baal Shem Tov
sat in his study
and received people who came to visit him,
seeking his guidance and advice.

For hours, he sat motionless.
People entered in small groups.
Two candles were set in front of the Besht.
An open book was placed on the table,
The *Sefer Yetzirah*,
which is the mystical Book of Creation.

Everyone who left that room felt
as if the Master had addressed him or her,
him or her alone,
as if nobody else had been standing there.

People discussed this when they were outside.
Each one of them insisted the Rebbe had spoken
to him or her exclusively,
And to no-one else in the room.

Then, they fell silent.

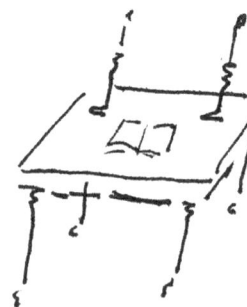

RABBI ISRAEL BEN ELIEZER OF MEDZHYBIZH (THE BAAL SHEM TOV)

HIS SECRET

A scholar in Satanow became trapped in his own web of strange theories and doubts. He read many books, including foreign philosophy and ideas that were contrary to Jewish beliefs, and asked himself many questions, like:

> *Does G'd exist?*
> *If so, Who is He?*
> *What is His definition?*
> *What is Truth?*
> *What was there before time started?*
> *Was there anything at all?*
> *Is everything one BIG illusion?*

He didn't discuss these thoughts with anybody. They were his secret.

When the Besht "saw" this scholar with his divinely inspired spiritual powers, from as far away as Medzhybizh, he ordered his coach-driver to prepare his wagon. The trip to Satanow was long and complicated, but the horses ascended and galloped by leaps and bounds through the sky, and the Master arrived in no time.

The Besht went straight to the place of the man who was torn apart by mountains of doubts and valleys of confusion. He entered the house without bothering to announce or introduce himself.

> "You," he pointed at the scholar, "are a most learned and highly educated man, and you wonder if there is a G'd!
> I, on the other hand, am a fool, and I believe!"

The scholar understood, that the Besht knew his deepest, most guarded secret.
Soon his doubt dissolved and the Secret revealed itself to him.

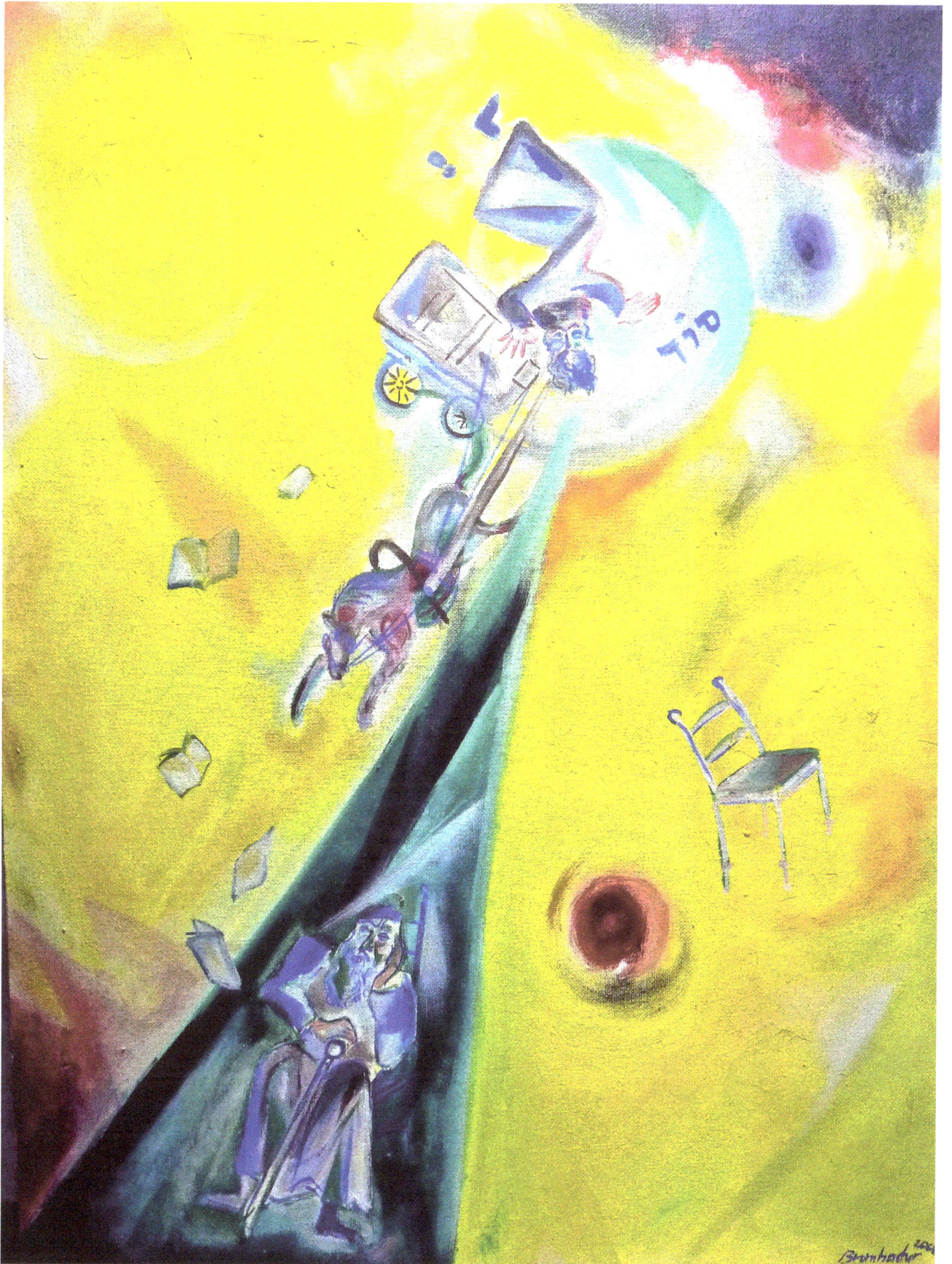

RABBI ISRAEL BEN ELIEZER OF MEDZHYBIZH (THE BAAL SHEM TOV)

IN A FIELD

A follower of Rabbi Israel Baal Shem Tov
planned to spend Yom Kippur in Medzhybizh,
In the Beis Midrash of the Master of the Good Name.
But, unfortunately, his wagon broke down on the way.
He was unable to reach Medzhybizh in time for Kol Nidrei.
Much to his chagrin, he had to daven—all alone—
next to his broken wagon, in a field.
He felt disappointed.
He felt cold, miserable, abandoned, depressed, and all alone.

He did not feel well at all!

       When he finally arrived at the Besht's house
         after the Holiday, in a bad and sad mood,
            the Baal Shem greeted
             him joyfully.

"Your
prayers," he
said, "flowed
from a sincere,
sad, and broken heart.
They lifted up all the
prayers of other wayfarers
and wanderers, prayers that were otherwise
doomed to linger in that field until the
end of time, unless they were redeemed."

RABBI ISRAEL BEN ELIEZER OF MEDZHYBIZH (THE BAAL SHEM TOV)

THE SIGNS

It is well known that the Besht had power over demons.
Once, the Master of the Good Name summoned Samael,
the Prince of the Demons, to appear before him.

Samael was furious! What nerve! What *chutzpah*!

Until now, he had been forced to appear only three times in history:
at the hour of the Tree in Paradise,
at the hour of the golden calf in the desert,
and at the hour of the destruction of the Temple in Jerusalem.

He refused to jump at the beck and call of a little Chassid
who called himself the Master of the Good Name.
What good name? Duh!

When the Besht found out how Samael thought about his summons,
he asked his students to bare their foreheads,
which bore the sign that HaShem had used to create man.

Now Samael felt compelled to show his presence.
He stood in awe and silence.
Now he obeyed the Baal Shem Tov.
He humbly asked the Master for permission,
however,
to linger a little bit longer,
to contemplate the foreheads
of those "Sons of HaShem."

RABBI ISRAEL BEN ELIEZER OF MEDZHYBIZH (THE BAAL SHEM TOV)

HE FULFILLS YOUR WILL

Yechiel Michal, a young Chassid,
went to spend some time with the Besht,
just so, out of curiosity.
He doubted if he wished to be a follower
of Rabbi Israel Baal Shem Tov,
and he didn't have a request for the Rebbe, either.

But when the Besht went on one of his trips,
he—surprisingly—took this young man
with him in his own personal wagon.
That was considered a big honor.

Twice, it seemed to Yechiel Michal,
that the Besht went in the wrong direction.
Twice, the young man made a sarcastic remark,
even though the Besht had told him earlier
that the road would reveal itself.

The Master asked the young man,

"Doesn't HaShem fulfill the will of those who fear Him?
Just look how He fulfilled your will.
You could make fun of me again!"

The remainder of the trip, Yechiel Michal was silent.

Later, he became a follower of the Baal Shem Tov.

And still later, he became the Rebbe of Zlozcow.

RABBI ISRAEL BEN ELIEZER OF MEDZHYBIZH (THE BAAL SHEM TOV)

THE TEFILLIN

Rabbi Israel Baal Shem Tov wanted to teach Rabbi Zvi Hirsh the Scribe
how to write *tefillin* with proper *kavanah* (intention).
One day, he promised the Scribe to take him into the woods
to show him HaShem's own Tefillin.

An other student of the Besht, Rabbi Wolf Kitzes, overheard this conversation.
His curiosity got the best of him,
and he decided to secretly follow along.
He wanted to see what would happen there in the woods.

When the two rabbis—with Rabbi Wolf Kitzes on their trail—
arrived at a clearing between the trees, they halted.
The Besht shouted in a loud voice:

"The Mikvah of Israel is HaShem!"

Suddenly, a flowing *mikvah* of spring water sprouted at their feet.
But Rabbi Wolf Kitzes eyes would witness no more . . .
The Besht, sensing that somebody was spying on him,
searched the nearby bushes.

He discovered his student,
Wolf Kitzes, cowering behind a copse.

RABBI ISRAEL BEN ELIEZER OF MEDZHYBIZH (THE BAAL SHEM TOV)

A RIVER

Once, a river which crossed the road to Medzhybizh—suddenly and unexpectedly— became
swollen and ~~~~~f~l~o~o~d~e~d~~~~~.
A pious woman, who used to bring the Besht and his Chassidim gifts, food and supplies,
was swept away and drowned.

Enraged upon hearing the tragic news, the Baal Shem Tov cursed the river,

and * it * dried ** up...

The soul of the river went up to the Heavenly Court to complain.
What was its crime? Don't rivers flood all the time? It's their nature.
Should they be punished for what is considered normal behavior for a river?
That made sense, of course.
Although the powerful curse of the Baal Shem Tov could not be reversed altogether,
the dried up river was granted permission to take revenge.
Somewhere in the future, it would swell one more time
and endanger the life of a relative of the Besht.
And on top of that, the Besht would be the only person in the world
who would be able to save that relative from drowning.

But for many years, nothing happened.
The dried up river had long been forgotten.
The Master of the Good Name had passed away.
He had long been buried.

Meanwhile, the son of the Baal Shem Tov had become a famous rabbi.
One night, he was traveling in the woods around Medzhybizh
and lost his way in the dark.
Without knowing it, he found himself at the banks of that old dried-up river.
All of a sudden—seemingly out of nowhere—
a gale

raged,

and

Ho *WL* E d!

Huge w **A** ve S~   u **P**

roSe ~

from ~~   the   dry
bedding!
They
quickly ~
~ dragged ~
~ **the** ~
poor ~~
~ *man* ~
~ into ~
the ~
depths. ~~~~

He was on the verge of drowning,
surrounded by blackness,
when he saw a bright lamp or fire piercing the clouds.

With all the remaining strength
that was left in his half dead body,
he
struggled   towards   the light,
and found   himself
—unexpectedly—wet,
miserable,
weak, exhausted,
but safe,
at the other side of the now rapidly slinking river.

That light was the soul of the Besht.

RABBI ISRAEL BEN ELIEZER OF MEDZHYBIZH (THE BAAL SHEM TOV)

A MOUNTAIN OF FIRE

The son of the Baal Shem Tov told the following story:

"After
my father
passed away, I
saw him in the
shape of a fiery mountain,

D
      I
        s
          P
            E   N
        S
      I
        N   g
   N   u   m
  E R   o
       u s   S
              P
      A
   R
     K
       s

When I asked him, why he appeared this way,
he answered me:

"This is how I served HaShem."

RABBI DOV BAER OF MEZRITCH (THE MAGGID OF MEZRITCH)

TO TIE HIS SHOES

Loeb ben Sarah's, the Itinerant Tzaddik,
spent some time with the Maggid of Mezhritch.
When Loeb's friends asked him upon his return
what he had learned, he answered,

"I didn't go to him to hear explanations of the Torah.
I went to see how he

                    t
                      ie
                        s
                          h
                          i
                          s
                            s
                              h
                                o
                                e
                                l
                                a
                                c
                                  e
                                    s.
                                      " 1

1 BT Shabbat 61a.

RABBI DOV BAER OF MEZRITCH (THE MAGGID OF MEZRITCH)

FIRE

The Maggid of Mezritch had passed away.
Everything which he had owned he had left to his son,
Avraham the Angel.
But all of the bequeathed items were later destroyed
when Avraham's house burnt down.
So, were all the famous Maggid's possessions gone, now?

No, because Avraham's brother-in-law
still kept the famous white *bekeshe*,
the Maggid's white Yom Tov robe, in his house.
He donated this robe to Avraham, as a gift.

On Erev Yom Kippur,
Rabbi Avraham wore the white *bekeshe*,
in honor of his father.

But not for long.

Leaning over,
he touched a candle.
The robe caught fire.
People quickly tore it off Rabbi Avraham's body,
but they were unable to save it.

The
white
bekeshe
was completely
consumed.

RABBI AVRAHAM THE ANGEL

A ROCK

It once happened, that Rabbi Avraham the Angel visited his father-in-law,
the Kremnitzer Rebbe.
He saw him standing near the window,
contemplating the mountain overlooking the town.

This took a long time…

One of the Chassidim in the room became impatient.
He asked the Rebbe
if he had never seen such a mountain before?

Ans-
wered
the Kremnitzer
Rebbe:
"I wonder
how such a
small rock
could puff itself

U P

to become such a
BIG MOUN-
TAI N !"

RABBI CHAIM MEIR YECHIEL OF MOGIELNICA

HIS OWN REBBE

Once, when he was a little boy, Chaim Meir Yechiel
came crying to his grandfather,
the famous Maggid of Koznitz.
The boy complained that his father had left the house to visit his Rebbe,
but that he, little Chaim, had no Rebbe whom he could visit.
The grandfather tried to console him,
"I am a Rebbe, you can come visit me!"

Now the little boy wanted to know
why grandfather visited an other Rebbe,
even though grandfather himself was a famous Rebbe?

"And why do you think I visit a Rebbe?", asked the Maggid curiously.
The child answered,
"At night, I see grandfather sitting in front of an old man,
like a servant in front of his master."
The Maggid explained to his grandson,
"That old man is the soul of the holy Baal Shem Tov.
He descended back into this world to console me.
When you are a bit older, you will be allowed to study with him as well."

The little boy shook his head.
"I don't want a dead Rebbe," he said softly.

Years later, after the boy had become the famous Rebbe of Mogielnica,
he declared that he had not changed his opinion.
A student and his Rebbe must have at least one thing in common:

a bodily garment.

This is the secret of the Shechinah in Exile.

RABBI MORDECHAI OF NESKHIZ

LIKE FISH

The
Neskhizer
Rebbe related

how **during** Elul,

the month **re**pentance,

his father, like many other

people, used to quote

Yechezkel the Prophet:

"Today is the day, that

the fish in the ocean

tremble !" [1] Someone

observed, "It is

more **accu**rate

to say that the

fi**sh in** the

waters

tre**mbl**e."

Said

the

Nes**kh**izer:

"What did he

mean?   It **was** the

se**cret** betwe   en HaShem

and **the** hu-   **man** souls."

---

[1] Ez.38:20

RABBI MORDECHAI OF NESKHIZ

HE MADE THE BED

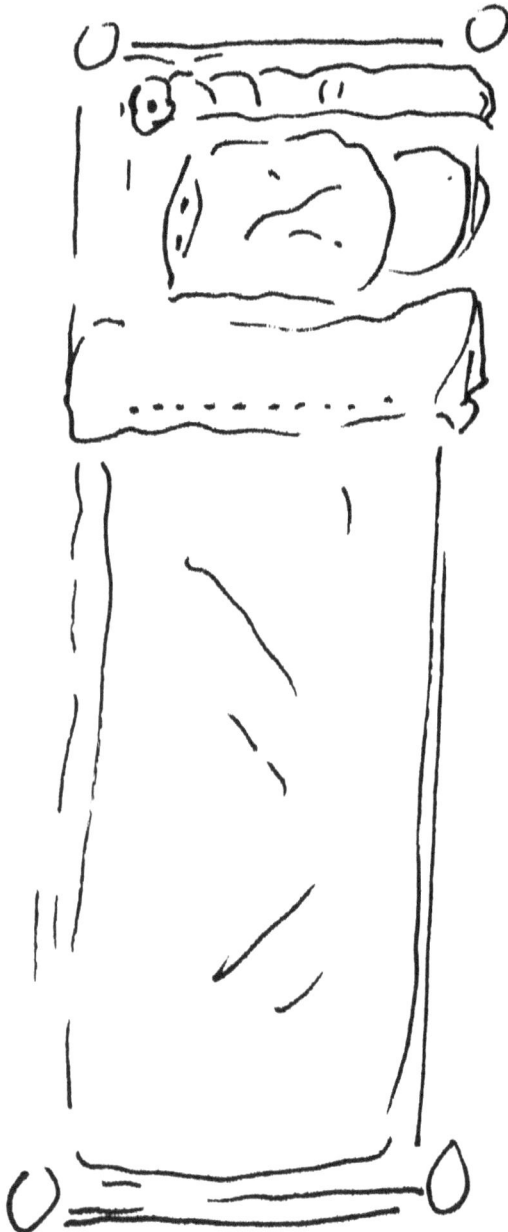

Once, the Neskhizer Rebbe visited a renowned, learned, and well-to-do friend, who was extremely humble.

The Neskhizer and his humble friend ate together. Then, they learned Torah together in the beautiful, big, comfortable brick mansion which belonged to this friend. When it was time to sleep, the wealthy friend himself—and not a servant—brought the Neskhizer to one of the many guest-rooms. Then he started to make the bed for his guest, all by himself. He didn't call a servant, although there were plenty of them in the house. Seeing the puzzled expression of the Neskhizer, he explained, "I do not do this for you. I do it for me."

RABBI SHMELKE OF NICHOLSBURG

A NEW RULE

Every newly appointed
rabbi in Nicholsburg
was requested to enter
a new rule, or custom,
into the chronicles of
the Jewish Community.

But Rabbi Shmelke…procrastinated.
He …hesitated.
He… dragged… his feet.
He postponed… to do it.
He… simply… avoided
complying… with this request.
He made up all kind of excuses,
until the secretary of the
Community pressed
him really hard.

Then   wrote
He   down
sat   the
down   Ten
and   Words.

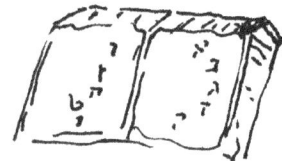

RABBI SIMCHAH BUNIM OF PSHISKHE

THE STRENGTH OF YOUTH

The story of the Akeda [1]
mentions specifically,
that Avraham and Yitzchak
went *sheneyhem be-yachad,*
the two of them together.

Why? Wasn't that already clear from the context?

Rebbe Reb Bunim explained:

"The test of the Akeda was much more difficult
for Yitzchak than it was for Avraham.

Avraham was told by HaShem Himself,
that He would provide a sacrifice.
Yitzchak, however, was told so by his father,
a mortal man of flesh and blood.

Therefore, Avraham wondered
why Yitzchak was so much stronger than he himself,
Avraham,
in dealing with this Akeda?

He figured, that there must be a connection
with Yitzchak's youthful age?

After this conclusion, Avraham forced himself
to feel like how he felt in his own youth.
And then they really went together."

---

[1] Genesis 22, the Binding of Isaac.

RABBI SIMCHAH BUNIM OF PSHISKHE

THE HIDDEN SHEPHERD

I saw Israel scattered upon the hills,
like sheep, which have no shepherd. [1]

Rabbi Simchah Bunim explained this verse as follows:

This does not mean that they have no shepherd.
The Shepherd is always present.

But when the sheep do not see Him,
they *think* that He is not present.

RABBI SIMCHAH BUNIM OF PSHISKHE

DUST AND WEALTH

After seducing Chava, the snake was cursed by HaShem,
Who ordered him to crawl on his belly and eat dust.

Rebbe Reb Bunim explained:

"Is that such a bad curse for the snake?
Filthy dust is everywhere!
Therefore, the snake has always something to eat!
But think about it this way:

Men earn their bread while suffering hardships,
They often feel that they are in dire straits.
Then they implore HaShem to help them.
Women suffer the pains and dangers of childbirth.
Often, they have to raise their kids in difficult circumstances.
Then they cry to HaShem for help.

Therefore, mankind has a strong relationship with HaShem.

But the snake has no reason to ask HaShem for anything.
The snake has no need for a relationship with HaShem.
He *has* no relationship with HaShem.

Is that the reason why some bad people are *filthy rich*? "

RABBI SIMCHAH BUNIM OF PSHISKHE

WE

Rabbi Simchah Bunim pondered over the plural *we* in the verse,
***We** will do and **we** will hear (listen)*,[1] which the
Jews exclaimed when they received the Torah at
Har Sinai. Why didn't all those people there
speak for themselves, saying, "I"?
You know what you personally will
accept or not, but how can you speak
for the people standing next to you?
Rabbi Simchah Bunim compared the Jews
at Har Sinai with a group of extremely
thirsty people. Somebody offers them
a cup of water. One person in the
group moans, "Please, give us
that cup,
we are
so
thirsty!"
Why does this person say,
"give us," instead of "give me?"

Because he knows, that everybody in his group is as thirsty as he is.
They all crave to drink that water just as much as he does.
Likewise, the Jews at Har Sinai knew
that all of them were thirsty for Torah.

No exceptions.

---

[1] Ex.19:8

RABBI SIMCHAH BUNIM OF PSHISKHE

I TEND YOUR SHEEP

After the "Holy Jew", Rabbi Yaakov Yitzchak,
had passed away, some Chassidim asked
Rabbi Simchah Bunim who would succeed him?
Rabbi Simchah Bunim didn't mention any names
but told them a story.

When a shepherd learned
that wolves had been spotted in the neighborhood,
he decided to stay with his sheep during the night,
to guard them in their meadow.
Being very tired, however,
he dozed off several
times.

The next morning, he woke up with a shock!
Frantically, he started counting his sheep.
To his tremendous relief they were all there,
alive and well.
He profoundly thanked HaShem,
exclaiming:

"Thank You! Thank You!
I am so happy!
Now give me *Your* sheep,
and I will take care of them like the apple of my eye!"

Rabbi Simchah Bunim was chosen as the new Rebbe.

RABBI SIMCHAH BUNIM OF PSHISKHE

THE ART OF DYING

When Rabbi Simchah Bunim
was lying on his deathbed,
his wife, Rivkah, cried bitter

     t

          e

     a

         r

     s.

He asked her,
"Why do you cry?"

Wasn't his whole life an attempt to learn how to die?

RABBI YISSACHAR BAER OF RADOSHITZ

YOU AND I   אתה

When Rabbi Shimon bar Yochai
and his son
were forced to hide for many years
in a cave in order to escape Roman persecutions,
Rabbi Shimon exclaimed,

"My son—you and I are sufficient for the world." [1]

Rabbi Yissachar Baer explained,
"That means: *'atta elokeynu,*
(**You** *are our G'd*),
and HaShem answers:
'ani ha-shem elokaykha,
(**I** *am the L'rd your G'd!*).

This **You** and **I** are sufficient for the world."

אני

---

[1] BT Shabbat 33b

RABBI ISRAEL OF RIZHIN

LETTERS AND VOWELS

Rabbi
     Israel of Rizhin compared Chassidim and Tzaddikim
                  to letters
                  and vowels.
                  For these
                  depend on
                  each other
                  for a good
                  understand-
                  ing of a text.
Chassidim elevate the Tzaddik, and the Tzaddik pulls his Chassidim with him to reach a higher level. Said the Rizhiner, "When

       one of my
         Chassidim
           travels in
             a coach to
            come visit
           me, he
          wants
          to sit
        on
     the

driving-box, next to the coach-driver. This way, he can request the driver to stop and jump off the wagon when it is time to daven Minchah, the afternoon prayer. But if there are Maskilim, modern secularists, in the coach, they complain and scream at the driver for this unwanted and "unnecessary" delay.

But wouldn't they experience a change of heart right there and then?"

RABBI ISRAEL OF RIZHIN

A TIN ROOF AND A TILE ROOF

It once
happened that
Rav Yaakov Ornstein
of Lemberg visited the Chassidic
Rebbe Israel of Rizhin. Rav Ornstein
wasn't fond of the Chassidic movement. He wanted
to prove that the Rizhiner wasn't a scholar. Therefore, he asked him
many complicated questions,
hoping that the Rizhiner would not know the
answer, or, even worse, give the wrong answer. However,
instead of answering the questions, the Rizhiner just wanted to know from
Rav Ornstein, "What material are the roofs in your town made of?" "Well, the
usual material, metal sheets,
mostly tin," answered
the puzzled Rav. Asked the
Rhiziner, "And why are they made
of tin?" "To protect the houses in case of a fire,
because metal does not burn." Said the Rizhiner: "In that case,
they could
have used clay tiles
as well." And he closed the
discussion, and left. Rav Ornstein didn't
understand the deeper meaning of this remark
and made fun of the Chassidic Master's response.
But when Rabbi Meir of Premishlan heard the story, he exclaimed:
"That is so
true! The heart of a
man who protects his community
is a roof, and it must be made out of clay tiles!
Why a roof or heart of clay? Because it is overwhelmed
by all the sorrows and grief of his people, it is permanently on the verge
of collapsing, it is breaking and shattering into shards!!! Yet it still endures! Yes! Clay!
But   what   kind   of   a   heart   would   be   made of   tin!?"

RABBI ISRAEL OF RIZHIN

HE DID NOT KNOW

When his Chassidim asked Rabbi Israel about the best way to serve HaShem, he told them that he had absolutely no idea.
When they looked puzzled, he told them the following story:

Two friends had been convicted of a crime.
They were sentenced to death.
The king knew the friends personally and was fond of them,
but even he, the king himself, couldn't overrule the sentence.
However, he could offer them one chance to save their lives.
They had to cross an abyss while balancing on a thin rope.
If they were able reach the other side, they were free.
If not, they would fall and crash to their death.

The first man ran fast and effortless across the rope.
He had crossed the abyss safely.
From the other side, his friend shouted,
"Tell me, quickly! How did you do that?"
The first man yelled: "I have absolutely no idea!
                    Every time I leaned
                              to one
                                        side,
              I quickly bent back
                                    to the other
                        side!
          And all of
                          a sudden
                I stood on firm
                                    grounds
                    again!"

Asked the Rizhiner, "You understand?"

THE DANCE

Once, on Simchat
Torah, the Chassidim of Rabbi Naftali were dancing outside, in
circles, and their Rebbe was watching
them from a window. All of a sudden he
raised his hand. They stopped. Rabbi Naftali
stood silent for a while, staring into the distan-
ce. Then he gestured them to continue, saying,
"When an officer falls in battle, shall the ranks of
the soldiers disperse and flee?" Later, the Chassidim discovered that exactly at the moment
they were told to stop, the Ulaner Rebbe,
who was a friend of Rabbi Naftali,
had
passed
away.

RABBI NAFTALI OF ROPSHITZ

A PLACE FOR STRANGERS PASSING THROUGH

During one of his many travels, the Ropshitzer happened to pass through a hamlet with a small graveyard. The few families that lived in the tiny village included only ten men over the age of thirteen. That was just enough to form a *minyan* - ten men required to recite communal prayers, like kaddish at a burial. The Ropshitzer asked the villagers, "What happens if one *minyan* man dies? Then there is no *minyan* anymore. And if no one dies, why do you need a cemetery?" Solemnly, a little girl stepped forward and answered the Rebbe, "The graveyard is only for strangers passing through." "That is right," mused the Ropshitzer, "the graveyard is only for strangers passing through…"

RABBI NAFTALI OF ROPSHITZ

CLOSED CURTAINS

The drapes in the house of the Ropshitzer were usually closed.
People could look, but not see into his room from the street.
Rabbi Eleazar of Koznitz, the grandson of the
Maggid, wondered - if you want people to
look into your house, why do you have
curtains? And if you don't want
them to look inside, why
have windows? When
the Ropshitzer asked
Rabbi Eleazar how
he had solved this
paradox, this is
what he answered:

"If you want
people whom
you love to
look into
your
house,
you
can
open
your
cur-
tains."

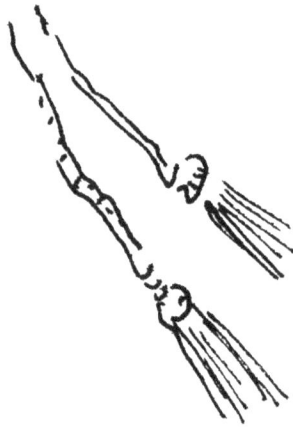

RABBI NAFTALI OF ROPSHITZ

JUST A LITTLE

A not overly bright student pored out
his heart in front of Rabbi Naftali.
Although he studied diligently,
he understood very little of what he read.

The Ropshitzer reassured him:

> "Don't worry!
> The mitzvah is to study,
> but it's not necessary to understand
> everything that you study.
> Neither is it required that
> you become a *talmid chacham*,
> a wise and learned man.

If your actions are improved
because of your studies,
then you have reached your goal —
even without understanding every text
and every paragraph which you have read
from the first till the last letter...

For it is written: *limdu haytav* (*learn to do well*)." [1]

---

[1] Jes.1:17

RABBI MENACHEM MENDEL OF RYMANOW

NO PEACE, NO QUIET

Unlike most travelers, Rabbi Mendel resented repairs and improvements of old roads
and the addition of many new, swifter routes.

What was the reason?

              Because bad,   roads
                        dilapidated

                                    forced
                                        travelers
        to   interrupt t
                            he ir
                                      traveling at
                              i
                          n ght.

They were compelled to seek lodgings at an inn.
There, they would meet other Jews,
eat together, discuss the shtetls they had visited,
talk about their families and their businesses,
smoke a pipe together,
ask around for a shidduch, a match, for their son, or for their daughter,
and speak words of Torah, as behooves a Jew.

       "But   now,"
          sighed   the Rymanover,
         "people   rush and
            hurry   day and
              night.   There is
                 no peace,   no quiet."

RABBI MENACHEM MENDEL OF RYMANOW

A COIN

Rabbi Mendel was extremely poor -
               like many Chassidim at that time.
More often than not he did not even
               have a dry crust of bread for his children.

One day, his little boy ran to him, crying out
               that he couldn't bear the hunger pangs anymore.
With a bleeding heart the father rebuked him,
               "If your hunger was really that strong,
HaShem would provide something to eat!"

               Still sobbing, the boy left the room.

After a moment, the father called him back, saying:

"I apologize to you, my dear child!
I didn't know how extreme your hunger was!"

202

RABBI CHAIM OF SANZ

IN THEIR OWN WAY

Said the Divrei Chaim, the Sanzer Rebbe,

"All Tzaddikim serve HaShem in their own way.

The person who states that *only his* rabbi is a Tzaddik,

Lo-

ses

both

Worlds."

RABBI MOSHE LOEB OF SASSOV

THE STICK

Rabbi Moshe Loeb did not grow up in a Chassidic family. On the contrary, his father strongly disapproved of Chassidim and their strange ways. But young Moshe Loeb ran away from home to study with Rabbi Shmelke of Nicholsburg. When his father found out what his son had done, he was furious.

He carved a
      big stick,
           and kept it
                ready
                    for the day
                        Moshe would
                            dare to come
                                home again.

Every time
   when the father found
      a bigger and better stick,
         he replaced the former one.

One day, the maid cleaned up the room and put the big stick in the attic. Just then, Moshe arrived. He had already heard about the stick and knew it was waiting for him. So, when his father looked around, Moshe climbed up to the attic, searched, found the stick, and handed it to his father.

They looked into
      each other's
         face for a long time.
            Then the father put
               the big stick to the side.

RABBI MOSHE LOEB OF SASSOV

A BABY BOY

A poor village woman had serious trouble while giving birth. The situation looked grim, even dangerous. The other villagers were afraid that she was on the verge of death. They decided to send a messenger to Rabbi Moshe Loeb in Sassov, begging for his assistance and intervention. Although the man traveled as fast as he could, it was a long road from his village to Sassov. He arrived in the middle of the night and knocked on the first lighted window he saw in the Jewish neighborhood. The owner of the house recognized a distressed Jewish traveler at his door and let him in. He asked the messenger why he had come to Sassov. Then he offered him a meal and a bed for the remainder of the night and advised him to go see Rabbi Moshe Loeb the next morning, because now it was night, too late to bother him.

All of Sassov was fast asleep.

At dawn, the owner of the house woke up the messenger and told him, that the woman in his village had delivered a healthy baby boy. Mother and child were doing well, *baruch HaShem*, blessed is the Eternal. The puzzled man thanked his host and walked outside. He asked people in the street where to find the house of the Rabbi. They all pointed at the house he had just left! When the messenger realized who the owner was of the house where he had spent last night, he was too embarrassed to go back. He mounted his horse and returned to his village.

There he found the healthy mother
and her healthy baby boy,
who had been born
at dawn.

RABBI MOSHE LOEB OF SASSOV

IN THE MIDDLE

Said the Sassover,

"Our path in this world is like the edge of a knife!

At this side is an abyss.   At that side is an abyss.

And

the

path

of

our

life

lies

right

in

the

middle."

RABBI MOSHE LOEB OF SASSOV

THE SINGING OF THE ANGELS

Rabbi
    Moshe
        Loeb
            was
                very
poor. His wife could barely afford to buy food. But, because she knew that
her husband really enjoyed drinking coffee, she bought him a tiny bag of
coffee beans every week. To make those precious beans last longer,
she made only one small pot a day. She placed the freshly brewed
coffee each weekday morning in her husband's study.
He loved to come home from shul and smell the delicious,
hot aroma wafting from the table. Now, it happened one time
that the rebbetzin had to leave the house to do an errand
right after putting the coffee pot in the study. A few
moments later, two Chassidim entered the house
to see Rabbi Loeb. When they did not find him
home, they sat themselves down in his study at
his table to wait for him. But Rabbi Loeb was
delayed and still in shul. The two Chassidim,
tired of waiting, helped themselves to the hot
pot of coffee. In fact, they finished the whole
pot and left. After a while, the rebbetzin
returned and discovered what had happened.
She was very upset! When Rabbi Loeb came
home, he tried to comfort her, saying,
"Don't be angry. Please forgive them! I know those two men! They
sing so beautifully, that they open my heart so I can hear the angels sing!"

RABBI MOSHE LOEB OF SASSOV

ONE HOUR

Said the Sassover:

"A
  man
    who
      can't
        call
          one
            hour
              of
                the

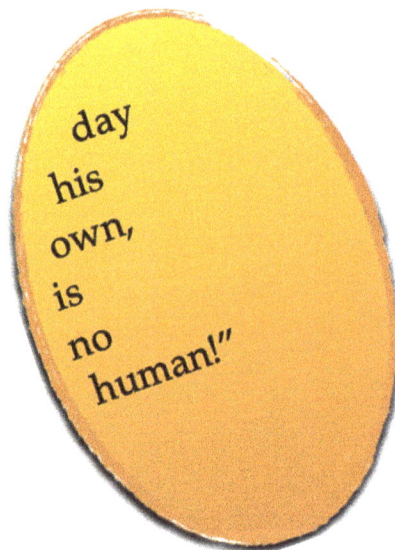

day
his
own,
is
no
human!"

215

RABBI MOSHE LOEB OF SASSOV

HERE LIVES A JEW

It is written:

For HaShem will pass through to smite the Egyptians, and when He sees blood upon the lintel and across the two posts, HaShem will pass over the door. [1]

Said the Sassover Rebbe,

"How come HaShem will *pass over*?

Isn't He omnipresent?

Is there any space in this world that is not filled with Him?

So you better read, *He jumps over*, or: *He hops over*,

because in all of the Egyptian houses HaShem saw death and grief.

But whenever He saw a Jewish house

He jumped for joy, and exclaimed:

"Here lives a Jew!'"

Upon hearing this,

Rabbi Moshe Loeb's host, Rabbi Elimelech of Lizhansk,

jumped

on

the   table

and

danced   around,

singing,

"Here

lives

a   Jew!   Here

lives

a

Jew!"

[1] Ex.13:23

RABBI NACHUM OF STEPINESHT

THE BASIC RULES

Once, Rabbi Menachem Nachum saw some of his students

                          play

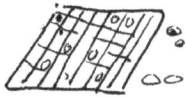

                     Check   ers
                 on   Cha
                    nu   kah.

He asked them, whether they knew the rules of the game?
But the boys were shy and felt embarrassed to answer such a simple question
— from such an important rabbi, no less—about a children's game.
Therefore, Rabbi Nachum answered his own question:

"There are three basic rules:

      don't go backwards;
                         don't take two steps at a time;
      and when you reach
                    the top of the board,
      you
            can
                go
      wherever
                         you
          want!

Remember this for the rest of your lives!"

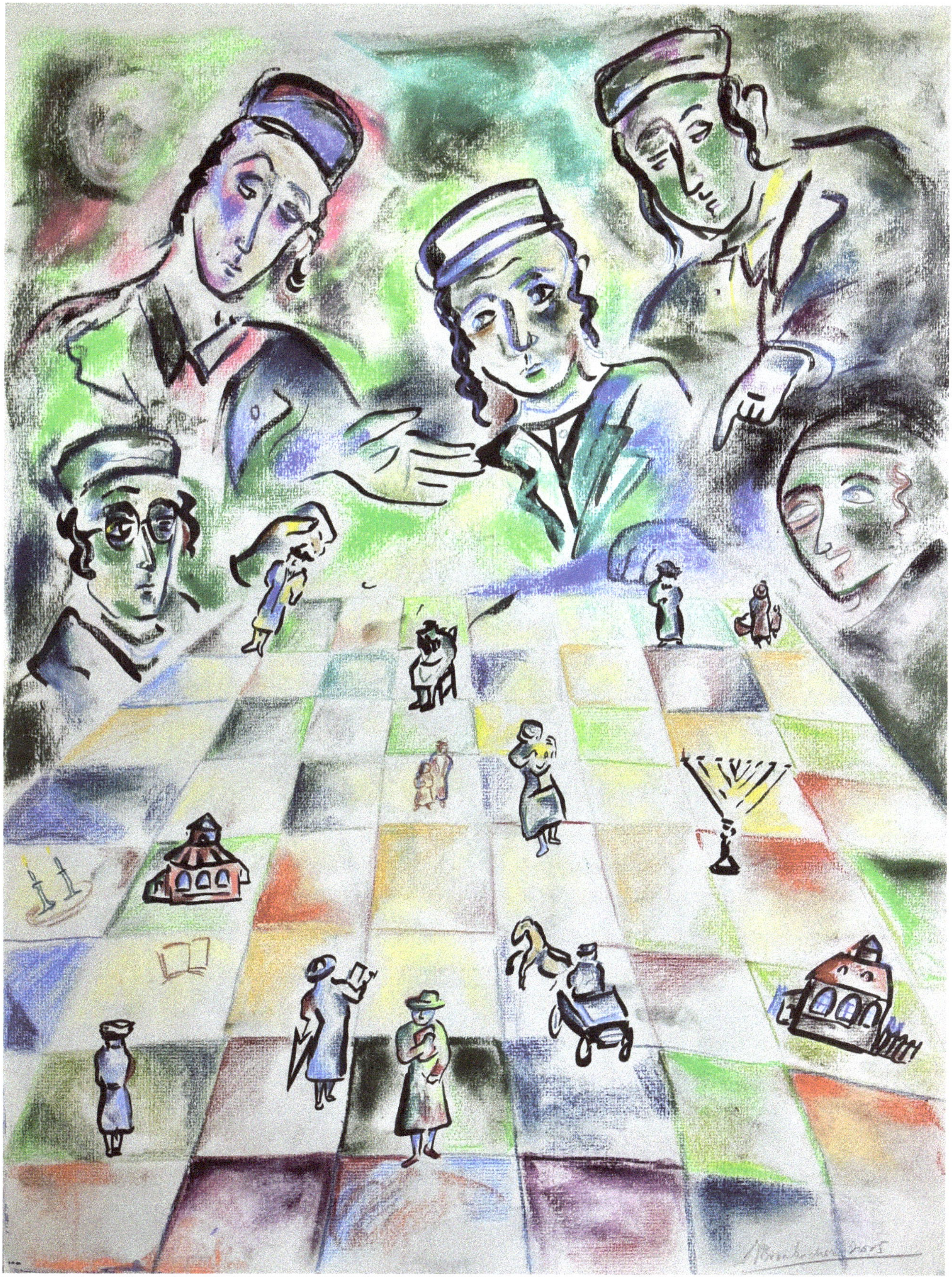

RABBI URI OF STRELISK

WITH A MINYAN

Rabbi Uri preferred to *daven* privately, by himself and in solitude, in his own study. Not in a noisy shul, where people inevitably talked, if not to him, then to each other, and where they distracted him. All these distractions led too many worshippers to loose *kavanah*, proper intention.

But then he studied about he importance of participating in communal prayer—in addition to hearing the Torah reading—and so, he decided to *daven* more often in shul. However, just like he had feared earlier, the community was not capable of *davening* the way he wanted - with the right intentions, intensity, and insight. Once again, Rabbi Uri preferred to stay home and *daven* in solitude.

But after hearing a *bat kol*, a *Divine Voice*, ordering him not to separate himself from the community, he gathered a *minyan* of handpicked Chassidim in his house and ended the practice of praying by himself.

He figured, "I will pray together with those men
of my *minyan* even if I don't appreciate their lack of
knowledge. Even if I don't have a high opinion of
their intentions. Because if H a S h e mhad ordered

me to	pray
together	with
ten	wooden
lecterns,	I
would	have
done	that."

RABBI YEHUDA ZVI OF STRETYN

A TRAPPED SOUL

Be- fore
he became
a famous
r abbi, the
Stretyner Rebbe
worked as a *shochet*, a ritual slaughterer.
He was a very successful
shochet! Cows ran to him and fowl flew to him, with
their necks stretched out, ready for his knife. One time, a goose
flew all the way from another town straight to Stretyn with the intention to be
slaughtered by him alone, and not by any other butcher! Why did these animals
behave in such an unusual manner? Because they knew that this
shochet, Yehuda Zvi in Stretyn, had the power to release
gilguls, reincarnated human souls which were trapped
in animal bodies. They were doomed to remain
gilguls until they did penance for their sins in earlier
lives, or were liberated by a Tzaddik. It happened one time,
that a huge ox went berserk. It broke loose, and bolted
straight into the woods. Now, everybody was afraid
of approaching that dangerous, fierce, and
ferocious animal, let alone catching it, so
they sent for Yehuda Zvi. He came, and
followed the trail of the ox. He found it
in the woods, resting near a copse,
peacefully chewing its cud. When the animal
saw the *shochet*, it stretched out its throat,
showing him it was prepared to be
slaughtered. Yehuda Zvi redeemed
its trapped soul with
one swift cut.

לשחוט האיל

RABBI MENACHEM MENDEL OF VITEBSK

PURE AND HOLY

Each of the students in the Beis Midrash of the Rabbi of Lubavitch,
the son of the son-in-law of the Alter Rebbe, used to place a candle in front of him
when he was studying.
But whenever the students told each other stories about Tzaddikim they extinguished
all but one candle.

Once, their Rebbe entered, and heard them talk about Rabbi Menachem Mendel of
Vitebsk.
He ordered the students to light all the candles again.

Why, they asked, if they were telling stories and not studying?

Answered the Rebbe,

"Because Rabbi Menachem Mendel
was such a pure and holy soul
that the sitra achra
(the realm of evil)
had no effect
on him
at
all."

RABBI YITZCHAK OF VORKI

NOT LONGER THAN THE ALEPH-BETH

Some Chassidim asked Rabbi Yitzchak of Vorki,
"Why is the *vidduy*, our confession of sins for Yom Kippur,
arranged according to the letters of the aleph-beth?"

He said to them:
"If it weren't for the
limited number of
letters in the
aleph-beth,
we would go on,
and on,
and on, and on,
and on,
and on, and on,
and on,
and on, and on,
and on
to confess
our sins,
for there is
no end
to sin
and to
the
knowledge
and
awareness
that
we
sin!"

RABBI MENDEL OF VORKI

IN SILENCE

Once, Rabbi Mendel of Vorki,
the son of Rabbi Yitzchak,
met with Rabbi Eleazar,
the grandson of the Koznitzer Maggid.

They sat together in a room
for a long time.

They didn't utter a sound.

Then they got up.

"Now we are ready,"
said Rabbi Mendel.

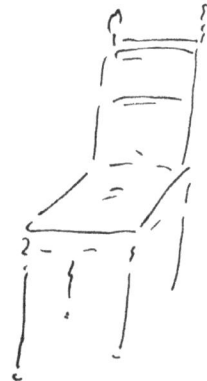

RABBI ZEV WOLF OF ZBARAZH

HIS FATHERS TEARS

Young Zev Wolf was a wild and unruly boy, *a wilde chaya,* who didn't give his parents much *nachas,* pleasure. He didn't like to study and he often got himself into trouble.

Some time before Zev Wolf's bar mitzvah, his father, Rabbi Yechiel Michal of Zloczow, went to a sofer, a scribe, to buy a pair of tefillin for his son. Before the sofer inserted the parchment into the "houses," the father asked him for the empty houses. He took them in his hand and stared at them for a long time, with a heavy heart. Tears dripped from his eyes into the houses. Then he handed them back to the scribe,

who inserted
    the parchment
and closed the
    houses by
stitching them
    up.

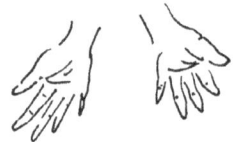

From the day that Zev Wolf started donning those tefillin, he changed. He wasn't wild anymore and studied diligently.

And after several years he became the Rebbe of Zbarazh.

RABBI ZEV WOLF OF ZBARAZH

TWO TZADDIKIM

During a fight
or dispute
between
chassidim
Rabbi Wolf
never favored
one party
over the
other.

He used to say,

"To me they are both equal!
Who would intervene with two tzaddikim?"

RABBI ZEV WOLF OF ZBARAZH

TALK TO IT!

Rabbi Wolf asked
his wagon-driver
not to whip the horse.

He said,

"You don't even have to shout at it,
if you know how to talk to it."

RABBI YITZCHAK EISIK OF ZHYDACZOW

HE DRAWS A CHORD

It is written in Gemara:[1]

Said Resh Lakish: Whoever occupies himself with Torah during the night,
the Holy One, blessed be He, draws over him a string of loving kindness
[to protect him] during the day, for it is said,
By day He does command His loving kindness,
and in the night His song is with me. [2]

This means, that in daytime the angels are silent
and Israel praises HaShem.
Resh Lakish also said, [3] that whoever occupies himself with Torah
in this World, which is like the night,
HaShem protects him in the World to come,
that is "by day."
And how does He do that?
By drawing a string of loving kindness over him,
for it is said: *By day He does...*

Young Yitzchak Eisik's father asked him:
"But don't we study Torah at night as well?
How come, then, that we are still oppressed, poor,
and living in miserable circumstances in daytime?"

The boy answered his father,
"This string of loving kindness is the fact that we still get up at night to study,
despite the fact that there seems to be no protection in daytime!"

---

[1] BT Chag.12b

[2] Ps. 42:9

[3] ibid.

RABBI ZVI HIRSH OF ZHYDACZOW

THE BIG CROWD

The Rabbi of Komarno once spent Shavuoth in the house of Rabbi Zvi Hirsh.

Early in the morning,
right before morning prayers,
he entered Rabbi Zvi Hirsh' study,
because he yearned to study Torah with him.

Rabbi Zvi Hirsh, however, didn't notice his guest's presence.
He was pacing back and forth the room
with a worried and absentminded expression on his face.

A few days later he explained to the Rabbi of Komarno
why he had been so worried.

He was afraid, he said,
that the big crowd of Chassidim
flocking to him for the Chag, the Festival,
had been sent by the demon
Samael,
In order to praise him excessively,
and to seduce him to become proud,
arrogant, haughty, and to make him boastful.

This was the thought that bothered him tremendously.

RABBI YECHIEL MICHAL OF ZLOCZOW

SUPPORT THE FAMILY

Rabbi Yechiel Michal was extremely poor.
The only income of his family was some small amount his wife received
from selling the milk of their only cow.

One Friday afternoon,
When Rabbi Yechiel returned home from the Beis Midrash,
he found his family in tears.
They were standing in a circle around their cow.
It was lying stiff on its side, on the cold ground, with its legs extend ended
and unable to move.
But somehow, there still seemed to be a flicker of life
lingering in the poor animal.
The rebbetzin had already sent for a farmer, to come and strip the skin.
The few coins she would get for the hide would be the very last support
from their beloved cow.

Rabbi Yechiel looked from the wretched shape on the floor
to the sad faces of his wife and children.
He gently prodded the animal with his cane.
"Don't you understand," he said in a soft, friendly voice,
"you have to feed this whole family -
all those little *yiddishe kinderlach*, they all depend on you!
Now, please, get up!"

The cow scrambled up and gave her milk again,
and the farmer, who had arrived to flay the carcass,
went home.

BRIEF BIOGRAPHICAL NOTES *about the rabbis in the stories.*
For more information see Sources and Literature.

R. Chanoch of Alexander: Rabbi Chanoch Henoch (1798-1870), the author of *HaShava LeTovah*, was the son of R. Pinchas HaKohen of Lutomirsk. He studied with R. Simchah Bunim of Pshiskhe and R. Menachem Mendel of Kotzk and served as a rabbi in Alexander (near Lodz) and Nowy Dwor. In 1866 he assumed leadership of the Gerer Chassidim. R. Chanoch tended toward mysticism and emphasized joy, happiness and the importance of singling out one particular mitzvah or character trait to work on. Personally, he refined his humility. He put internal worship on one line with Torah study and stated that every mitzvah done "from within" strengthens a person. The devotion with which it is done causes a transformation that brings about Divine Emanation. Chassidim and their Rebbe strongly depend on each other. The work *Siach Sarfei Kodesh* includes stories about Rabbi Chanoch.

R. Zusha of Anipol: Rabbi Meshullam Zusha, aka Rebbe Reb Zusha (1718-1800) was the younger brother of R. Elimelech of Lizhansk, aka the Noam Elimelech, a friend of R. Shneur Zalman of Liadi (the Alter Rebbe), and a student of the Maggid of Mezritch, next to whom he was buried. Suffering from ill health, R. Zusha was destitute all his life. Still, he remained deeply pious and used to say: "Whatever comes from HaShem is good." He wrote no books of his own, but stories about him are included in *Menorat haZahav*. Reb Zusha was succeeded by his son, R. Zvi Menachem Mendel. The Ostroger Rabbi which is mentioned in "A Cold Sukkah" is R. Meir Margoliouth (d.1790).

R. Avraham Yehoshua Heshel of Apt: (Opatow), aka the Ohev Yisrael (1755-1825) was a student of R. Elimelech of Lizhansk and R. Yechiel Michal of Zloczow. He served as a rabbi in different towns before he settled first in Apt, and later in Medzhybizh. He valued Torah study and promoted the dissemination of Chassidut. His work *Ohev Yisrael* is a commentary on the weekly Torah portions.

R. Shalom of Belz: Rabbi Shalom Rokeach, aka the Sar Shalom (1779-1855) was a descendant of R. Eliezer Rokeach of Amsterdam. Orphaned at an early age, he was raised by his uncle, R. Yissachar Baer Ramraz of Sokal. Rabbi Shalom studied with the Chozeh of Lublin, R. Avraham Yehoshua Heshel of Apt, the Maggid of Koznitz, and R. Uri of Strelisk. He combined Torah scholarship with Chassidut before this was a generally accepted path. He valued Kabbalah, composed niggunim, but authored no books. His teachings were collected in *Midbar Kodesh* and *Dover Shalom*.

R. Levi Yitzchak of Berditchev: (1740-1810) was an *illuy* (child prodigy). He was a student of R. Shmelke of Nikolsburg, who sent him away to study with the Maggid of Mezritch. The Berditchever officiated as a rabbi in different towns before he settled in Berditchev. He emphasized love for HaShem and one's fellow Jews (*ahavat yisrael*), and is probably best known for his arguments with HaShem on behalf of the Jewish people. He authored *Kedushat Levi* (on the weekly Torah portions) and a commentary on *Pirkei Avot*.

R. Nachum of Chernobyl: Rabbi Menachem Nachum Twersky (1730-1797) was a student of the Baal Shem Tov and the Maggid of Mezritch. After he lost his parents, his uncle sent him to an anti-Chassidic yeshivah and supported him to become a *melamed*. Instead, he became a Chassidic *maggid*. He valued Lurianic Kabbalah, joy in prayer, eagerness to do mitzvoth, and giving *tzedakah*. He wrote *Meor Einayim*.

R. Meir of Dzikow: R. Meir Horowitz (1819-1878) was a halachic authority and belonged to the school of Ropshitz. He studied with his father, R. Eliezer of Dzikow, and R. Chaim of Sanz, and became a Rebbe during his father's lifetime, which is highly unusual. He conducted a wealthy, splendorous Court. R. Meir authored three works all named *Imrei Noam*: one on the Torah, one on Festivals, and one volume of responsa.

R. Yitzchak Meir of Ger: R. Yitzchak Meir Rothenberg (or Rothenburg) Alter, aka the Illuy of Warsaw or the Chidushei HaRim (1799-1866) was a descendant of the Maharam and the grandfather of the Sefat Emet. His father studied with the Berditchever and was a friend of the Koznitzer Maggid, which influenced his upbringing. R. Yitzchak was a student of R. Simchah Bunim of Pshiskhe and R. Menachem Mendel of Kotzk. In 1859 R. Yitzchak Meir became the leader of the Gerer Chassidim. He was a great Talmud scholar who emphasized Torah study. His book *Chidushei HaRim* is popular in both Chassidic and non-Chassidic circles.

R. Yitzchak Itzik of Kalev: (Kallo/Kallov), R. Yitzchak Itzik Taub, aka the Singing Tzaddik (1751-1821) composed many niggunim and was one of the first Chassidic rabbis in Hungary. After being introduced to Chassidism by Loeb Sarah's, he studied with R. Shmelke of Nikolsburg and R. Elimelech of Lizhansk. He loved the mystical aspects of Torah and emphasized the value of intense prayer and staying humble (and simple) despite being highly educated.

R. Aharon of Karlin: unlike most Rebbes, R. Aharon Perlov (HaGadol, 1736-1772), grew up relatively wealthy. He studied with the Maggid of Mezritch, R. Shmelke of Nikolsburg, R. Elimelech of Lizhansk, the Berditchever, and was a good friend of the Chozeh and R. Menachem Mendel of Rymanov. Recognized as a Talmudic and kabbalistic scholar, miracle-worker, preacher, and healer, he emphasized enthusiasm for Chassidut. Despite his frail health he led an ascetic life and secluded himself to improve his relationship with G'd. He authored *Avodat Yisrael* (on the weekly Torah portions) and homiletical works on the *Zohar* and *Tehillim*.

R. Moshe of Kobryn: R. Moshe ben Yisrael Pol(i)yer (1784-1858) studied with R. Mordechai of Lechowitz. He was extremely modest and valued the important bond between the Tzaddik and his Chassidim, humility, truthfulness, and repentance, and urged his Chassidim to refrain from complaining in bad situations. He loved telling stories and *meshalim* (examples). His teachings are collected in *Amarot Tehorot*.

R. Pinchas of Koretz: R. Pinchas ben Avraham Abba Shapiro (1726-1791) was a descendant of R. Nathan Shapiro, the author of *Megalleh Amukot*. R. Pinchas' father strongly opposed Chassidism, but after meeting the Besht, he and his son became the Besht's most ardent followers. According to the Baal Shem, a soul like Pinchas' soul descends into the world only once every five hundred years. R. Pinchas was a student of the Maggid of Mezritch but he settled eventually in Koretz. He set out to Tzfat but died while he was still in Russia. R. Pinchas valued the *Zohar*, *devekut*, singing niggunim, honesty, humility, love for one's fellow Jews (*ahavat yisrael*), and rejection of pride and arrogance. He recommended fasting to overcome evil impulses. His sermons were collected in several works, e.g., *Midrash Pinchas*.

R. Yisrael of Koznitz: R. Yisrael Hapstein, aka the Koznitzer Maggid (c.1738-1814) was born after the Besht gave his poor and childless parents a blessing. He was as student of the Maggid of Mezritch, R. Shmelke of Nikolsburg, R. Elimelech of Lizhansk, the Berditchever, and a friend of the Chozeh of Lublin and R. Menachem Mendel of Rymanov. The Maggid was an accomplished Talmudic and kabbalistic scholar— influenced by the Maharal—a *baal mofet*, healer, and famous preacher (*maggid*). He strove to solve the problem of the *agunah*, the "chained wife". His contacts in the Polish community enabled him to soften the effects of antisemitic policies. The Koznitzer valued *devekut* in davening, enthusiasm, and communion with HaShem. The Tzaddik must lead his Chassidim in divine worship through his devotion and bring them closer to G'd, because a Chassid is unable to reach that high level of the Tzaddik by himself. The Koznitzer wrote several works on subjects like the *Zohar*, *Tehillim*, Chassidism, and homilies: *Beit Yisrael*, *Or Yisrael*, *Ner Yisrael* and *Avodat Yisrael* (on the weekly Torah portions).

R. Menachem Mendel of Kotzk: R. Menachem Mendel Morgenstern (1787-1859), the author of *Ohel Torah* and *Emet VeEmunah*, was a child prodigy (*illuy*) with a non-Chassidic background. He was a student of the Chozeh of Lublin and R. Simchah Bunim of Pshiskhe, whom he eventually succeeded, and the teacher of the Izbicer Rebbe. R. Menachem Mendel hated falsehood and hypocrisy. He secluded himself from the outside world for twenty years.

R. Chaim of Krosno: (Krasnoye, d.1793) belonged to the circle of the Besht and was a friend of R. Pinchas of Koretz and R. Menachem Mendel of Vitebsk. He considered the shipwreck which ended his voyage to Eretz Yisrael as a sign of Divine anger, and demanded that just the words *"He was not worthy to visit Eretz Yisrael"* be written on his gravestone. R. Chaim left no works of his own.

R. Mordechai of Lechowitz: (Lechowicz), R. Mordechai ben Noach (1742-1810) was a student of R. Aharon of Karlin, R. Baruch ben Yechiel of Medzhybizh, and R. Shlomo ben Meir HaLevi of Karlin, with whom he went into exile after confrontations Mitnaggedim, who even had him imprisoned by the authorities after accusing him of spreading Chassidut in Lithuania. R. Mordechai was a funds-collector for Eretz Yisrael. He stated that the Tzaddik must help and support his Chassidim in all fields, but more than anything else he must instill in them the fear of Heaven.

R. David of Lelov: R. David ben Shlomo Biderman (1746-1814) studied with the Chozeh, R. Elimelech of Lizhansk, and R. Moshe Loeb of Sassov. Earning his livelihood as a grocer, he became interested in Kabbalah and Talmud. He valued *ahavat yisrael*, always willing to help his fellow Jews, and was convinced that no Jew can be a real sinner. He used to frequent the market square to feed animals whose owners forgot about them while they were drinking at the inn. The Lelover tried to reconcile the Chozeh and the Holy Jew of Pshiskhe, but didn't succeed.

R. Shneur Zalman of Liadi: aka the Baal haTanya or Alter Rebbe (1745-1812) is the founder of Chabad Chassidism (an acronym of the kabbalistic *sefirot* **CH**ochmah, **B**inah, **D**aat). He succeeded the Maggid of Mezritch, who had initiated him in Lurianic Kabbalah. The Alter Rebbe was imprisoned after accusations of

Mitnaggedim from the circle of the Vilna Gaon and settled later in Liadi. He stated that there are few *tzaddikim* (righteous people) but many *baynonim* (average people, between good and bad). The latter need the help of a Tzaddik in their strife for perfection. He preferred involvement in practical mitzvoth over theoretical problems and emphasized Torah study, meditation, and joy, because it banishes sin-inducing melancholia. Evil and temptation must be fought with the help of the "hidden love" that resides in the heart of every Jew. The Alter Rebbe wrote several influential works, such as *Likutei Amarim* (or *Tanya*), *Likutei Torah, Torah Or, Iggerot Kodesh, Sefer HaMaamarim, Boneh Yerushalayim, Meah Shearim, Hilchot Talmud Torah* and *Shulchan Arukh haRav*.

R. Yaakov Yitzchak of Lublin: R. Yaakov Yitzchak Horowitz, aka the Chozeh or the Seer of Lublin (1745-1815) was called the Seer because he had visions and glanced at people's forehead to "see" their thoughts. He was a student of R. Elimelech of Lizhansk, the Maggid of Mezritch, the Berditchever, and R. Shmelke of Nikolsburg. He spread Chassidism all over Poland. Many of the Rebbes mentioned in this book were his students. Numerous anecdotes are told about miracles he performed, his mysticism, and his theory of Napoleon being the harbinger of messianic times. The Chozeh valued *ahavat yisrael* and fulfilling people's basic material needs before talking with them about spiritual values. He authored *Torat HaChozeh MiLublin*, which is a compilation of several other works.

R. Loeb ben Sarah: not much is known about this Itinerant Tzaddik Aryeh Loeb (Leib) Sarah's (Loeb ben Sarah, c. 1730-1791), who based the use of his mother's name instead of his father's name, Yosef, on *Sefer Raziel*. His mother had married an older widower to escape the attention of a gentile landowner and was rewarded for her modesty with an exceptional son, Aryeh Loeb. He was a student of the Maggid of Mezritch and the Besht, who told him to support the Lamed Wowniks (Thirty-six Hidden Tzaddikim), to raise money for good causes, and to travel. Loeb Sarah's emphasized improving one's personal conduct and assisting prisoners. He did not set up a Court or found a dynasty.

R. Yisrael ben Eliezer Baal Shem Tov of Medzhybizh: aka the Baal Shem Tov, Master of the Good Name, Besht, or Rivash (c. 1698-1760) is considered the founder of the Chassidic movement. Orphaned at an early age, he lived in poverty, worked as a teacher's helper, and frequently retreated into the Carpathian Mountains to meditate before he revealed himself as a leader. In 1740 he founded a Beis Midrash in Medzhybizh. The Besht left no systematic teachings. His followers spread his words and doctrines. He was a miracle worker and mystic, who emphasized G'd's omnipresence, and *devekut* (communion with G'd) through ecstasy, singing, dancing, and joy. He loved his fellow Jews tremendously (*ahavat yisrael*), and appealed particularly to the poor, ignorant masses in Eastern Europe. There are several early collections of stories about the Besht, like *Shivchei HaBesht* and *Sefer Baal Shem Tov (Al HaTorah),* and modern collections by Martin Buber and Maggid Yitzchak Buxbaum, in addition to numerous studies and anthologies.

R. Dov Baer of Mezritch: aka the Maggid of Mezritch (1704?-1772) studied in a mitnaggidic (anti-Chassidic) yeshivah in Lemberg (Lvov) and became a poor *melamed*, like his father. After meeting the Besht, he became a Chassid and studied Kabbalah. His fame as a preacher earned him the title "The Maggid," without the need to add his name. He succeeded the Besht despite the seniority of another beloved student, Yaakov Yosef of Polonoye. Unlike the Besht, R. Dov Baer—who suffered from bad health—did not travel. He stayed in Mezritch, where he successfully promoted Kabbalah in Chassidism and serving G'd in poverty. He left no books. His teachings are preserved in *Maggid Devarayv LeYaakov, Or Torah*, and *Or HaEmet*.

His son, **Avraham the Angel,** (1740-1776) was a mystic and kabbalist. He wrote *Chesed LeAvraham*. He was know called "the Angel" because he lacked appetite, like an angel, and because his father had such a pure *neshamah* (soul) when he begat him, that the soul of an angel entered the unborn child. He favored seclusion and fasting.

R. Chaim Meir Yechiel of Mogielnica: R. Chaim Meir Yechiel Shapira, aka the Saraf of Mogielnica (1796-1849), was a grandson of the Koznitzer Maggid. Upset about the unfavorable political climate for Jews in Russia and Poland, he urged his Chassidim to relocate to Eretz Yisrael. R. Chaim valued prayer and frequently drew up a will before praying, because he feared that he might not survive his own enthusiasm, for which he was called the Saraf (Burning Angel).

R. Mordechai of Neskhiz (Nesukhoyshe): aka the Rishpei Esh (d.1800) became a merchant despite his rabbinic lineage as a descendant of Don Yitzchak Abravanel. The Rishpei Esh studied with R. Yechiel Michal of Zloczow. He was a mystic and miracle worker, and tried solving the problem of the *agunah*. His work has been published together with that of R. Yitzchak of Neskhiz in *Toldot Yitzchak*.

R. Shmelke of Nikolsburg: R. Samuel Shmelke Horowitz (1726-1778), the author of *Divrei Shmuel, Imrei*

Shmuel, and *Shemen HaTov,* was the oldest son of R. Zvi Hersh of Chortkow. He claimed that he had inherited the soul of his biblical namesake and ancestor, Samuel the Prophet. R. Shmelke was a staunch adversary of Chassidism before he met the Maggid of Mezritch. When he served as a rabbi in Nikolsburg (Mikulov, in Moravia), together with R. Elimelech of Lizhansk, he solved a community controversy about "too much Chassidut in Nikolsburg."

R. Simchah Bunim of Pshiskhe: R. Simchah Bunim Bonhart, aka Rebbe Reb Bunim (c. 1767-1827) was introduced to Chassidism by his father-in-law, a *maggid.* He studied with R. David of Lelov, the Chozeh of Lublin, the Koznitzer Maggid, and R. Moshe Loeb of Sassov. Before becoming a Chassidic Master, R. Simchah Bunim, the manager of a timber producer and a pharmacist, wore modern clothes. He was influenced by the writings of he Maharal and favored an intellectual approach to Torah study. He admired his fellow student of the Chozeh, R. Yaakov Yitzchak the Yehudi (the Holy Jew), whom he accompanied to Pshiskhe. R. Simchah Bunim succeeded the Kotzker Rebbe. He valued Torah study, sincerity, and introspection, frequently abandoning fixed prayer times, postponing prayer till he felt that he was mentally ready. In his old age, he continued studying despite his diminished eye-sight. He greatly influenced the schools of Vorki and Alexander. His students collected his teachings in *Kol Simchah, Niflaot R. Bunim, Ramatayim Tzofim* and *Chedvat Simchah.*

R. Yissachar Baer of Radoshitz: R. Yissachar Baer Braun, aka the Saba Kadisha, the Saintly Zayde of Radoshitz (Radishitz, 1765-1843) used to be a trader with the nickname Berel the Batlan (Idler). Considering this life a mere stage before the Real (Next) World, he did not care about his grinding poverty. He studied with R. Elimelech of Lizhansk, R. Moshe Loeb of Sassov, the Chozeh, and visited the Koznitzer Maggid. The Yehudi (the Holy Jew) liked him so much, that he called him "my own Berel," and wanted to teach him the language of the birds. R. Yissachar Baer, a miracle worker, was beloved among Gentiles as well, who considered him a prophet. He emphasized self-sacrifice, which enables a person to serve HaShem in many different ways. He valued fixed prayer times and regular visits to a Tzaddik. He strongly opposed the secular Haskalah movement, assisted cantonists, and collected the discourses of Yehoshua Heshel of Apt in *Torat Emet.*

R. Yisrael of Rizhin: (Ruzhin) R. Yisrael Friedman (1797-1850), the great-grandson of the Maggid of Mezritch, the grandson of Avraham the Angel, the son of R. Shalom Shachna, and the father of R. Nachum of Stepinesht, was ordained as a rabbi at the tender age of fifteen. Because the Besht had stated that his (the Besht's) soul would linger in this world for another forty years after his death, some believe that it descended into the Rizhiner. Although he maintained a splendorous Court, the Rizhiner did not enjoy his wealth but fasted, put hard peas in his shoes, and went without sleep. After being falsely accused and imprisoned in Kiev, he escaped to Sadagora. R. Israel valued tolerant, kind behavior and hospitality. His discourses are collected in *Beit Yisrael* and *Niflaot Yisrael.* He authored *Irin Kaddishin, Keneset Yisrael* and *Beer LaYesharim.*

R. Naftali of Ropshitz: R. Naftali Zvi Horowitz (1760-1827) was a student of the Chozeh, the Maggid of Koznitz, R. Menachem Mendel of Rymanov, and—in particular—R. Elimelech of Lizhansk. His family was not Chassidic and his mother came from Hamburg (Germany). R. Naftali is known for his wisdom and wit, his niggunim, and kabbalistic knowledge. Out of modesty he tried to conceal his extreme piety. He considered faith superior to wisdom. Since the Torah starts with a *b/veth* and ends with a *lamed,* thus forming the word *lev* (heart), one must serve HaShem above all with the heart. R. Naftali strongly opposed Napoleon's secular, modern, anti-religious, assimilationist policies. He founded several smaller Chassidic dynasties and authored *Ohel Naftali, Ayalah Sheluchah* and *Zera Kodesh.*

R. Menachem Mendel of Rymanow: (c.1745-1815), the author of *Ilana DeChayyei, Menachem Tzion* and *Divrei Menachem,* was a miracle worker. He got frequently trapped in conflicts between Chassidim and Mitnaggedim. He studied with the Maggid of Mezritch at the tender age of eleven, with R. Shmelke of Nikolsburg, R. Elimelech of Lizhansk, and was a friend of the Chozeh and the Koznitzer Maggid. R. Menachem was very ascetic and renowned for his extraordinary awe of HaShem, passion in prayer, and his rules regarding modesty for women's apparel. Like the Chozeh, he believed that the Napoleonic wars announced messianic times and the final Redemption.

R. Chaim of Sanz: R. Chaim Halberstam, aka the Illuy of Tarnograd (Torongrad, 1793-1876), the Divrei Chaim, or Light of the Exile, and the author of the responsa *Divrei Chaim,* was a descendant of the Maharshal and Chacham Zvi. He studied with R. Naftali of Ropshitz and visited the Rizhiner. R. Chaim became a Chassid after he met the Chozeh, who predicted that he would become a Master. As a *posek* and scholar he emphasized humility. At the question why he loved poor people so much, he simply answered: "HaShem loves them." Because of R. Chaim, some spell Sanz as **Tz**anz, with a tzade, because he is a **Tz**addik.

R. Moshe Loeb of Sassov: R. Moshe Loeb Erblich, aka the Ohev Yisrael (1745-1807), was a student of R. Shmelke of Nikolsburg, the Maggid of Mezritch, and Elimelech of Lizhansk. He was a Talmudic and kabbalistic scholar and spread Chassidut in Galicia. The Sassover loved all Jews, but in particular poor, oppressed and simple folks, which earned him the title Father of Widows and Orphans. He loved to dance, composed niggunim, and was a prolific author (e.g., *Likutei ReMaL*). His thoughts were published posthumously in *Chiddushei ReMaL*.

R. Nachum of Stepinesht: R. Menachem Nachum Friedman, (Stefanesti, Romania, 1823-1869) was the fourth son of R. Yisrael of Rizhin. He was a miracle worker and kabbalist, but gave no public Torah lectures. Preoccupied with the arrival of Moshiach, he prepared a special room in his house to receive and honor him with a golden crown and other attributes.

R. Uri of Strelisk: R. Uri ben Pinchas, aka HaSaraf (1757-1826), studied with R. Shlomo HaLevi of Karlin and visited R. Elimelech of Lizhansk, R. Pinchas of Koretz, and R. Zusha of Anipol. R. Uri was opposed to miracle workers and strove for high ethical standards. He and his followers were poor and despised wealth. Because of his ecstatic prayer and various facial expressions for different tasks, like prayer or study, he was named Saraf (Fiery Angel). His teachings are collected in *Imrei Kodesh*, *Sefer Imrei Kodesh HaChadash*, and *Or Olam*.

R. Yehudah Zvi of Stretyn: R. Yehudah Zvi Hersh Brandwein (1780-1830) belonged to an old rabbinic family. He was the beloved student of R. Uri of Strelisk, whom he succeeded, and studied with R. Shlomo HaLevi of Karlin. He valued ecstasy in prayer. His teachings are collected in *Degel Machaneh Yehudah*, *Sheerit Yehudah Derekh Chaim*, and *Tokhachat Musar*.

R. Menachem Mendel of Vitebsk: (or Horodok, 1730(?)-1788) studied with the Maggid of Mezritch but returned to Vitebsk after the Maggid's passing. After Mitnaggedim imposed a *cherem* (verdict of religious expulsion) on Chassidim, he and R. Shneur Zalman of Liadi tried to reconcile both groups, but the Vilna Gaon refused to see them. R. Menachem Mendel was a *mekubbal* (kabbalist). In 1777 he left Lithuania to settle in Tzfat, where he experienced conflicts with Mitnaggedim as well. He founded the first Chassidic community in Eretz Yisrael and died in Tiberias. He didn't consider himself a Tzaddik who was entitled to give blessings to people. He valued *devekut*, *kavanah*, and making HaShem the abode of the world—not the other way around. He emphasized fear of sin instead of fear of punishment and worshipping HaShem through corporeality. The reward of a mitzvah is the mitzvah itself. He authored *Peri HaAretz*, *Peri HaEtz*, *Etz Peri*, *Likutei Amarim*, and a collection of letters, *Nefesh Menachem*.

R. Yitzchak of Vorki (Warka): R. Yisrael Yitzchak Kalish, aka the Ohev Yisrael (1779-1848) was a student of R. Simchah Bunim of Pshiskhe, R. David of Lelov, and the Chozeh. Together with the Gerer Rebbe and the Rebbe of Alexander he belonged to the friends of the Kotzker. Renowned for his gentleness and rectitude, he gathered many students. He pleaded with the government about the plight of the cantonists, and met with Moses Montefiori to find a solution for the many oppressive antisemitic decrees in Russia. Some of his teachings are collected in *Ohel Yitzchak* and *Chuzzak Chen*. One of his sons founded the Amshinover dynasty. His second son, **R. Menachem Mendel Kalish of Vorki**, aka the Silent Tzaddik (1730-1868) didn't like to study in his youth but changed in later years. Seclusive and ascetic, R. Yitzchak's only spoke words of Torah, and then only if he felt that he could not stop his heart from overflowing. He stated that a man must obtain an erect bow, a silent cry, and a motionless dance. Alcohol helped him to love HaShem more and gave him joy.

R. Yitzchak Itzik of Zydaczow: (1795-1873), the author of *Likutei Maharia* and *Likutei Torah VeHaSha"s*, was a nephew and student of R. Zvi Hersh of Zydaczow, and visited the Rebbes of Sanz, Strelisk, Ropshitz, and Dzikow. Mainly interested in Lurianic Kabbalah, he lived an ascetic life of poverty. R. Aharon of Chernobyl called him the Mirror Without Blemish.

R. Zvi Hersh of Zydaczow: R. Zvi Hersh Eichenstein (1763-18310), a non-chassidic Torah scholar and *mekubbal*, turned to Chassidism, and studied with R. Elimelech of Lizhansk, the Chozeh, R. Moshe Loeb of Sassov, and R. Baruch of Medzhybizh. Because he considered Chassidism and Kabbalah to be closely interwoven, he used Chassidism as a tool to achieve the goals of the Lurianic Kabbalah of the Ari. He was the teacher of R. Yitzchak Itzik of Komarno and R. Meir Leib b.Yechiel of Michael, the Malbim. R. Zvi Hersh is the founder of the Zydaczow dynasty and the author of *Sur MeRa VeAseh Tov* (an introduction to *Peri Etz Chaim* of the Ari), *Peri Kodesh Hillulim*, *Ateret Tzvi* (on the *Zohar*), *Beit Yisrael* (on the Torah), *Kuntres HaShemot*, and *Sefer Tzvi LeTzaddik*.

SOURCES AND LITERATURE for further reading:

-Ben Amos, D. and Mintz, J. (1993). *In praise of the Baal Shem Tov (Shivhei HaBesht)*. Northvale NJ: Aronson Publishing.

-Boteach, S. (1996). *Wisdom, Understanding, and Knowledge. Basic Concepts of Hasidic Thought*. Northvale NJ: Aronson Publishing.

-Buber, M. (1947). *Tales of the Hasidim. The Early Masters*. New York: Schocken Books.

— (1961). *Tales of the Hasidim. The Later Masters*. New York: Schocken Books.

— (1999). *Gog and Magog*. Syracuse: University Press.

-Buxbaum, Y. (2005) *The Light and Fire of he Baal Shem Tov*. New York: Continuum Press.

-Dalfin, H. (1995). *Demystifying the Mystical: Understanding the Language and Concepts of Chasidism and Jewish Mysticism*. Northvale NJ: Aronson Publishing.

—(1996). *To Be Chasidic*. Northvale NJ: Aronson Publishing.

—(1999). *Farbrengen: Inspirational stories and anecdotes*. New York: Otsar Sifrei Lubavitch.

—(2013). *Habad Portraits: Interesting People, Events, and Curiosities in Habad Hasidism: Volume I.* Boulder CO: Albion-Andalus Books.

— *Chasidic Niggunim* (Audio tapes). New York: jewishinfo.org

-Finkel, A.Y. (1996). *The Great Chassidic Masters*. Northvale NJ: Aronson Publishing.

-Gurary, N. (2000). *The Jewish Holy Days in Chasidic Philosophy*. Northvale NJ: Aronson Publishing.

-Himelstein, S. (1991). *A Touch of Wisdom, A Touch of Wit*. New York: Mesorah Publications.

-Kantor, M. (1990). *Chassidic Insights. A guide for the Entangled*. New York: Naran Chai Publications.

-Klein, E.(1995). *Meetings with Remarkable Souls*. Northvale NJ: Aronson Publishing.

-Lamm, N. (1999). *The Religious thought of Hasidism*. New York: Yeshiva University Press.

-Newman, L.I. (1987). *Hasidic Anthology*. Northvale NJ: Aronson Publishing.

-Polski, H.W. and Wozner, Y. (1989). *Everyday Miracles. The healing Wisdom of Hasidic Stories*. Northvale NJ: Aronson Publishing.

-Rabinowicz,H.M. (1988). *Hasidism, The Movement and its Masters*. Northvale NJ: Aronson Publishing.

-Rabinowicz, T. (1989). Chassidic Rebbes. *From the Baal Shem Tov to Modern Times*. Southfield Mich.: Targum/Feldheim Press.

---The Encyclopedia of Hasidism. (1996). Northvale NJ: Aronson Publishing. *(N.B.: this work has a very good bibliography)*

-Raskin, A.L. (2003). *Letters of Light: A Mystical Journey Through the Hebrew Alphabet*. New York: Sichos in English.

-Sadeh P. ed. (1987). *Sippure HaBesht*. Jerusalem: Karta. (*in Hebrew)*

-Shochet J.I. (1990). *Chassidic Dimensions. Themes in Chassidic Thought and Practice*. New York: Kehot Publication Society.

-Steinsaltz, A. (1988). *The Long Shorter way. Discourses in Chasidic Thought*. Northvale NJ: Aronson Publishing.

-Wiesel, E. (1984). *Souls on Fire and Somewhere a Master.* Suffolk: Penguin Books.

— (1978). *Four Hasidic Masters and their Struggle against Melancholy*. London: University of Dame Press.

-Zevin, S.Y. (1981). *A Treasury of Chassidic tales on the Festivals*. Jerusalem: Artscroll.

GLOSSARY

Achia of Shilo: biblical prophet during the reign of King Solomon (I Kings 11-14 e.a.) with an exceptional lifespan (BB 121b). Being an expert in Kabbalah, he became the mystical teacher of the Besht.

Agunah: a "chained" wife, abandoned by her husband who either disappeared without divorcing her, or whose death could not be confirmed. Therefore, she is not allowed to remarry and—especially in the olden days often—condemned to a life of poverty.

Ahavat yisrael: love for one's fellow Jew, even if s/he is uneducated or shows repulsive behavior. This love is an important principle in Chassidism.

Akeda(h) (or *Akedat Yitzchak)*: the binding of Isaac (Genesis 22).

Amalek: a descendant of Esau who tried to harm the Jews in the desert (Exodus 17 e.a.). His name became a synonym for persisting anti-Semites.

Ari (za"l): acronym of Rabbi Yitzchak ben Shlomo Luria (1534-1574), the Ari haKadosh (Holy Lion) who resided in the kabbalistic city of Tzfat. He was the founder of the Lurianic system in Kabbalah which has influenced Chassidism deeply.

Ark (aron): 1. the wooden portable receptacle containing the Tablets with the Ten Commandments, which was placed in the Mishkan (Tent) in the desert and later in the Beit haMikdash (Temple) in Jerusalem. 2. The ornamental closet or niche containing the Torah scrolls in the synagogue.

Avraham Avinu: Avraham our Father, the biblical Patriarch Abraham.

Baal mofet: miracle worker. Many Chassidic Rebbes carried this title.

Bar Mitzvah: "Son of the Law," a Jewish boy's transition at age thirteen from childhood to religious responsibility, like being included in a *minyan* and donning *tefillin*.

Bat Kol (in Yiddish Bas Kol): a Divine Voice, a mystical Voice from Heaven.

Beit haMikdash: the Temple in Jerusalem. The first Beit haMikdash was built by King Solomon and destroyed by the Babylonians in 586 b.c.e.. It was rebuilt, and destroyed by the Romans in 70 c.e. The third Temple will be rebuilt in messianic times. This holy Sanctuary contained the Tablets of the Law.

Beis (ha)Midrash: house of study or study hall, often serving as a place to eat or sleep for poor traveling students as well. The Beis Midrash plays an important role in Chassidic life.

Bekeshe: coat or robe worn on Shabbat and Yom Tov.

Beth Din, Beis Din: rabbinic court. Because the local secular authorities in Eastern Europe were often hostile towards Jews, the Beth Din did not only handle religious matters but civil cases between Jews as well.

Bochur: unmarried young man who studies in a Yeshivah and often lives there as well. Poor bochurs were often supported by the community and /or rich people, invited for meals, and given clothes.

Challah, challoh, plural: challoth/challes: braided Shabbat loaf over which a special blessing is said on Shabbat and Tom Tov. Usually two loaves are required.

Chag: one of the three Biblical Holidays: Pesach, Shavuoth and Sukkoth.

Cantonist: a young Jewish boy forcibly drafted in the Russian army of the Czar for up to 25 years. This robbed him from receiving a Jewish upbringing and becoming a "good Jew". Many cantonists died young due to the hardships of army life and some were baptized. Many Chassidic Rebbes tried to ransom cantonists by bribing the authorities or—if that was not possible— assisting the hapless kids in other ways.

Chanukah: The Festival of Lights in winter. It commemorates the miracles that were performed during the anti-Hellenistic revolt in 167 b.c.e. Children play special games, like checkers and spinning tops.

Chassid, plural Chassidim: "pious, faithful person," a follower of the Chassidic movement founded by the Baal Shem Tov, see the introduction.

Chesed: (act of chesed) "kindness," particularly a mitzvah or deed done to help people physically or materially. *Chesed* is very important in Chassidism. Everyone can perform acts of chesed, it does not require education or wealth.

Choson/chatan: bridegroom.

Chozeh: a seer, one who has the mystical, G-d given ability to read people's thoughts and fate by looking at their foreheads and has visions of events happening in a different time and place.

Chutzpah: impudence combined with fearlessness and lack of respect.

Daf: a leaf in a volume of Gemara. The front and back side make two pages. The front side is called daf a, the back side daf b, e.g., 12a or 23b. All volumes, however, start with daf 2a. There is no "leaf 1".

Daven: to pray.

Devekut: "clinging" to HaShem, the Chassidic principle of a Master's communion with G'd and his contemplation of G'd, which can be obtained through prayer, singing, etc., and even through seemingly mundane acts which are transformed into holiness through the intentions of the Chassid.

Dvar Torah: lecture on a religious subject, words of Torah.

Eliahu haNavi: the mystical Biblical prophet Eliahu (Elijah, ninth century b.c.e., see 1 and 2 Kings). He never died, but ascended to Heaven in a chariot of fire. He travels in disguise through the world to help people, and teach and assist those who study Torah or Kabbalah with the right intentions. Eliahu is the subject of many legends and stories.

Elul: the autumnal month preceding Rosh haShanah (New Year), a special time for repentance (*teshuvah*) and introspection.

Eretz Yisrael: the (holy) Land of Israel.

Erev: the day preceding a Jewish Holiday or Shabbat, as well as the evening the Holiday itself starts, e.g., Erev Shabbat is both Friday in daytime, when preparations are made for Shabbat, and Friday evening itself after Shabbat has already begun.

Esrog (ethrog), plural Esrogim (ethrogim): citron, a lemon-like, fragrant fruit that is used on Sukkoth as part of the "four species." See Lulav.

Fathers and Mothers: the biblical Patriarchs and Matriarchs, Avraham, Yitzchak, Yaakov, Sarah, Rivkah, Leah and Rachel.

G'd: Orthodox Jews do not spell the Ineffable Name (Tetragrammaton) of G'd in full. Even in English, a dash or apostrophe substitutes one letter. G'd is called *HaShem*, The Name, or Ado-nay, my L'rd.

Galut: see *Golus.*

Gan Eden: Paradise, Garden of Eden.

Gartel: a long sash wrapped around the waist to separate the "animalistic" part of the body from the head and the heart. It is always worn during prayer and often the whole day.

Gefilte fish: stuffed carp, a popular Shabbat dish.

Gemara (Gemore): the Talmud (which consists of Mishnah and Gemara), the Oral Law given on Mount Sinai together with the Written Law (the Five Books of the Torah). The Gemara consists of 64 treatises in Hebrew and Aramaic, dealing with every aspect of life, science, the supernatural, etc. To study Gemara properly requires a lifetime.

Gilgul: a reincarnated soul who is denied entrance to the Next World because of unfinished business in this world, often as a result of a sin, and must stay in limbo. Being incorporeal and, therefore, unable to repent, such souls often get permission to return into the body of an animal, a human being, or even inanimate objects. They can be redeemed by their own actions or by the action or blessing of a Tzaddik, after which the soul finally gets permission to enter the Next World.

Golus, Galut: Diaspora, the Great Exile and dispersion of the Jewish people which started after the destruction of Jerusalem and the first Temple in 586.b.c.e., and increased after the destruction of Jerusalem and the second Temple in 70 c.e. This exile will come to an end when Moshiach will gather all exiled Jews and bring them back to a rebuilt third Temple in Jerusalem.

Hadassim: myrtle twigs, part of the "four species" used on Sukkoth. See "Lulav".

Halachah: the vast body of Jewish laws, (legal) obligations, and prohibitions in every aspect of life.

Har Sinai: Mount Sinai, where HaShem handed the Torah to Moses (Moshe Rabbenu).

HaShem: literally, the (ineffable) Name, the Tetragrammaton, which out of utter respect may not be pronounced, but is substituted by "The Name."

Haskalah: the movement of the Jewish Enlightenment. It began with Moses Mendelssohn in the eighteenth century in Germany. Influenced by Napoleon's principles of "Freedom, Equality and Brotherhood," the movement strove for equal rights and civil status for the Jews in their respective non-Jewish societies. It promoted assimilation to the Gentiles in dress, customs, and education, the abolishment of religious laws and prohibitions that set Jews apart from gentiles—such as *kashrut,*—giving up Yiddish in favor of languages like German, Polish or Russian, and abandoning Torah study in a Yeshivah in favor of a secular (University) education. The Chassidic movement ardently fought the strong influence of the Haskalah on young people.

Illuy: child prodigy.

Kabbalah: mystical, esoteric system explaining the Torah, including cosmology, numerology and metaphysical descriptions of the supernatural. Studying Kabbalah is usually restricted to male Torah scholars who are married and over forty years old. The Lurianic Kabbalah (see: *Ari*) greatly influenced Chassidism.

Kallah: bride.

Kavanah: devotional intention, the yearning and desire to study, fulfill mitzvoth, and pray with fervor. This is an important principle in Chassidism, see the introduction.

Keruvim: Cherubs, the winged creatures placed on top of the lid of the Ark with the stone Tablets (Exodus 37:7-9).

Kiddush: the blessing over a cup of wine and/or two *challot* at the beginning of a meal on Shabbat and Yom Tov.

Kugel: a heavy noodle or potato pudding, a popular Eastern European Shabbat dish.

Kvitl: a written request for help, a blessing, advice, financial aid, etc., presented by a Chassid to a Tzaddik. It is usually accompanied by charity money, which the Tzaddik uses to assist the poor in his community.

Lashon hara/hora: slander and gossip, which are considered a great sin.

Lulav: palm leaf. The word is used *pars pro toto* for a bundle of the "Four Species": willow twigs, myrtle twigs, a palm leaf, and an *esrog* fruit. The *lulav* is an essential attribute for the autumnal Festival of Sukkoth (Leviticus 23 e.a.)

Maariv: the evening prayer.

Machzor: prayerbook for Holidays and Festivals.

Maggid: an inspirational preacher. Eastern European traveling preachers delivered their sermons and homilies all over the country and were quite influential. Rabbis usually stayed in their own town and made legal decisions, but did not preach. The Maggid of Mezritch was such an exemplary preacher, that he is generally known as "The Maggid."

Maskil, (plural Maskilim): a follower of the *Haskalah* movement, an assimilated, non-religious Jew who dresses in modern clothes and does not keep kosher or observes Shabbat.

Matzah, matzoh, plural matzot/matzos: the flat, unleavened Pesach "bread" made of flour and water. It is eaten in remembrance of the slavery in Egypt. All leavened food, such as bread, is forbidden on Pesach.

Mayses: (Yiddish, from Hebrew *maaseh*), stories.

Melamed: a Hebrew teacher for young boys in a *cheder* (religious elementary school). A *melamed* was usually neither respected nor well paid.

Mekubbal: a kabbalistic scholar, a rabbi who is involved in Kabbalah.

Mikvah: a ritual bath to spiritually (and physically) cleanse oneself. In Chassidism, it is important for men to immerse every day and before saying specific prayers.

Minchah: the afternoon prayer.

Minyan: a quorum of ten Jewish males over the age of thirteen (Bar Mitzvah age). Certain prayers or Torah readings in the synagogue cannot take place without the presence of a *minyan*.

Mitnaggid/Misnaggid, plural Mitnagdim/Misnaggedim: an "opponent," of the Chassidic movement, usually with a Lithuanian-style religious background which favors rigorous scholarly Talmud study (see the introduction). N.b., although the Maskilim opposed Chassidism as well, they are not called Mitnaggedim.

Mitzvah, mitzvoth: a religious commandment in the Torah (like saying the appropriate blessing over food, or Shabbat). Often, "mitzvah" is also used in the sense of a "good deed," like helping somebody (see *chesed*).

There are 613 mitzvoth in the Torah. The (heavenly) reward for performing a mitzvah is simply being able to perform that mitzvah.

Moshiach: the descendant of King David who will redeem the Jews from Exile, rebuild the Beit haMikdash (Temple) in Jerusalem, and restore an ideal, theocratic reign in Israel. The final Redemption and arrival of Moshiach can be accelerated by doing mitzvoth and studying Torah. Some Chassidic Masters, such as the Besht, were able to go up to Heaven to inquire why Moshiach had not arrived yet.

Naches, nachas (nachat): the pleasure one derives from one's children, particularly in a Jewish religious sense.

Name: one of the many mystical and secret Names of G'd which have special powers, hence the "Master of the Good Name" for a Tzaddik using these Names effectively in prayer to accomplish favors for the Jewish people.

Neshamah: the soul, specifically, the divine soul that dwells in every Jew.

Niggun, plural niggunim: a melody, often hummed without words or with meaningless syllables like *ba-ba-ba-bom-bim*, composed by Chassidic Masters to help them meditate and become closer to G'd; see the introduction. Sometimes the syllable *du* (Yiddish: you) refers to HaShem.

Pels: (Yiddish) fur or fur-coat.

Pesach: a Festival in spring commemorating the liberation of the Jews from their slavery in Egypt followed by their Exodus, which in turn led to receiving the Torah on Har Sinai and entering Eretz Yisrael, as described in the Book of Exodus. Pesach has a special spiritual meaning. It urges a person to liberate him/herself from their own spiritual "Egypt". During eight days, only unleavened food—like *matzah*—is permitted. On the first two evenings, a special meal, the *seder*, is conducted, and the story of the exodus is told.

Plotz: (Yiddish) to explode.

Posek: a rabbinic authority who makes binding decisions in controversies concerning Jewish Law.

Prince of Fire: one of the angels in charge of fire. Several Chassidic Masters, like the Baal Shem Tov and Reb Zusya of Anipol, were able to contact or summon angels and demons.

R., Rabbi: often abbreviated as R. (followed by a name), a spiritual and religious authority who studied Jewish Law in a Yeshivah and has been ordained by one or more other rabbis. Although most Chassidic Masters were rabbis, this is not a *conditio sine qua non*.

Reb: respectfully, "sir," "mister," (e.g., reb Zusha, Mr. Zusha).

Rebbe: Chassidic leader, Tzaddik; see the introduction.

Rebbetzin: the wife of a rabbi.

Rosh haShanah: the Jewish New Year which celebrates the creation of the world on the first two days of the autumnal month of Tishri. During this solemn Festival people are inscribed in the Heavenly Book of Life and the *shofar* (ram's horn) is blown. It is followed by the "Ten Days" of repentance and introspection. The Book with one's fate—with the exception of one's attitude and fear of Heaven—is sealed on Yom Kippur. Rosh haShanah and Yom Kippur together are called the High Holidays.

Ruach Shabbat/Shabbos: the spirit or atmosphere of Shabbat.

Samael: one of the names of Satan, the impure Prince of Demons. He seduced Eve (Chavah) by hiding in the tree with the forbidden fruit and led the Jews astray by hiding in the Golden Calf (Pirke de Rabbi Eliezer 45).

Seder: the ceremonial meal on the first two evenings of Pesach. It includes reading the Haggadah, the book which commemorates the liberation from Pharaoh and Egyptian slavery, and eating matzah and bitter herbs. In Chassidic circles, this meal has a strong messianic meaning, bringing about the Final Redemption.

Sefer: a book containing Scriptures in a broad sense, or religious subjects, such as Torah commentaries.

Sefer Yetzirah: the *Book of Creation*, an early mystical work on cosmology and the creation of the world. It is very popular in Chassidic and kabbalistic circles.

Shabbos(dik): (related to) Shabbos (Shabbat), the seventh day of the week, on which G'd rested from creating the world. Shabbat, from Friday at sundown till Saturday at night, is a day reserved for spiritual matters. Many types of work are forbidden. People go to shul (synagogue) and serve a delicious meal at home.

Shavuoth: the biblical Festival in summer, seven weeks after Pesach, to celebrate the harvest and the day that

Moshe Rabbenu received the Torah on Mount Sinai and handed it to the Jewish people.

Shechinah: the Divine Immanence in this world. After the destruction of the Temple, she accompanied the suffering Jewish people into the Great Exile (*Golus*) in order to assist and support them. She is often depicted as a Heavenly Bride waiting to be reunited with her Divine Groom.

Shidduch: a match. Chassidic marriages were usually arranged by the families, often with the help of a *shadchan*, a professional matchmaker.

Shimon bar Yochai: a Tanna, Talmudic teacher and rabbi from the second century c.e. He and his son went into hiding from Roman persecutors in a cave for several years. There, they studied Torah buried up till their necks in the sand to preserve their worn-out clothes for times of prayer.

Shlep: (Yiddish), toil.

Shochet: a ritual slaughterer. Animals that have not been slaughtered by a *shochet* are not kosher and are not permitted for consumption by observant Jews.

Shofar: a ram's horn. It is blown at special occasions and Festivals, such as Rosh haShanah.

Shalom bayis: the harmonious relationship of a couple (or family) and the peaceful atmosphere in their home.

Shtibel, shtiblakh: (Yiddish: a little room), a small, unofficial shul, often located in a living room or a house. Many Chassidic Rebbes had their own *shtibel*.

Shul: (Yiddish: school), a synagogue, often combined with a study hall.

Simchah: "joy," a Jewish festivity with a party and a meal, like a wedding or a Bar Mitzvah.

Simchat Torah: a joyous Festival in autumn right after Sukkoth, to celebrate the annual cycle of reading the Torah. Led by the two "grooms" of the Torah, people dance around with the Torah scrolls in the synagogue—and sometimes the street—in between ending the old cycle and starting the new one.

Sitra achra: (Aramaic), literally, "the other side," a euphemism for the world of demons, (spiritual) impurity, devils, and evil.

Sofer: a scribe of Torah scrolls, *tefillin* and *mezuzoth* (a Torah text fixed to the doorpost).

Shtraymel: the traditional fur-hat worn by Chassidim on Shabbat and Yom Tov. Each group has a slightly different model. Wearing a *shtraymel* (or *spodek*, a different model) has a mystical meaning and significance.

Sukkah: a temporary hut or booth with a roof made of branches or reeds, reminiscent of the Biblical huts in the desert made after the Exodus. During the Festival of Sukkoth Jews eat and—if possible—sleep in their *sukkah* during the week of the Festival.

Sukkoth/ Sukkos: the joyous biblical Festival in autumn to celebrate the harvest and to commemorate the journey through the desert after leaving Egypt on Pesach. The main customs for Sukkoth are waving a Lulav and dwelling in a *sukkah*.

Tallis (tallith): a four-cornered prayer shawl with ritual fringes with knots (*tzitzit*).

Talmid chacham: a religious scholar, Talmudic scholar.

Tefillin: phylacteries, small black boxes (called: "houses") containing Torah texts. *Tefillin* are strapped around the forehead and the (left) arm during certain prayers (see Deuteronomy 6:8).

Tzaddik, *plural*: **Tzaddikim**: "a righteous man," a charismatic spiritual leader (Rebbe) of a group of Chassidim; see the introduction.

Tzedakah: charity, financial assistance for the needy. The word *tzedakah* shares the same root as *tzedek*, righteousness, because financial wealth comes from G'd and should be divided in a fair way among all people.

Tish: (Yiddish: table), a festive meal of a Tzaddik and his Chassidim, an important Chassidic custom; see the introduction.

Ushpizin: the seven Biblical, mystical guests who visit the *sukkah* during the seven nights of the Festival of Sukkoth: Avraham, Yitzchak, Yaakov, Yosef, Moshe, Aharon, and David.

Viduy: the alphabetical confession of sins. This prayer plays an important role in the liturgy of Rosh haShanah and Yom Kippur.

Yahrzeit: (Yiddish, **Yohrzeit**), the anniversary of somebody's passing. People say special prayers and perform other memorial acts, like lighting a candle and giving *tzedakah*.

Yam Suf: the Red Sea, which G'd parted for the Jews to escape Pharaoh's soldiers (Exodus 14).

Yeshivah: a rabbinical college, a higher institution of Jewish learning.
Yiddishe kinderlach: (Yiddish, endearing), "little Jewish children".
Yom Kippur: the Day of Atonement, which occurs ten days after Rosh haShanah. This is the most solemn day in the Jewish year. People fast, confess their sins, and pray for forgiveness.
Yom Tov: a (biblical) Jewish Holiday.

About the illustrations:

Originally, this book was illustrated with ink drawings made by the artist in 1999. Some of them have been included. Later, the artist added new pastel and ink drawings and used some of her older work to create this colorful edition of the stories. For more information about the stories and the art, please contact the author/artist, Shoshannah Brombacher, at: shoshm@gmail.com or on Facebook.
www.absolutearts.com/portfolios/s/shoshannah

About the Author/Artist

Shoshannah Brombacher (b.1959) is an author, artist, scholar, and *maggidah* (story teller) from Amsterdam. She holds a Ph.D. from Leyden University (Holland) in Medieval Hebrew Poetry and researched the seventeenth century Sephardic Community of Amsterdam. She has participated in and contributed to research projects on Jewish manuscripts, books, and tombstone inscriptions. She has taught and performed research in Leyden, Amsterdam, Jerusalem and the Free University of Berlin. She recently moved back from Brooklyn to Berlin, where she dedicates her time to art, writing, lecturing, and telling Chassidic stories, and states that, "For me, family and art are inseparable parts of my Jewish life. My academic background brings deeper meaning to my art, understanding of life and devotion to HaShem. The teachings of the Chassidic Masters fascinated me since I discovered them in my father's study long ago." Brombacher's paintings are a tribute to the Chassidic way of life and service to HaShem, which spread light in a dark world and enrich our hearts and minds.

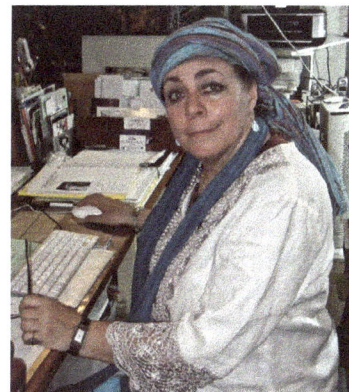

Some of the stories in this book have been published (in a slightly different version) on the website of Chabad: chabad.org, and some of the drawings were used as cover art or illustrations by different authors.
Brombacher has participated in many international art exhibitions and won several awards for her work. Other books by the author include scholarly editions and:

• *The Little Rose on the Mountain* (about the rose in Jewish texts, with many illustrations),
• *Painting the Dybbuk. Between Two Worlds. Ansky's Play seen through an Artist's Lens;*
• *The Golem in Brooklyn: The Golem Exhibition at the Brooklyn Jewish Art gallery at CKI;*
• *Pictorial for The Story of My Life. Various Events and Episodes of an Orphan By Pinkhes- Dov Goldenshteyn: Seen through the eyes of an artist.*
• *Haggadah shel Pesach-The Passover Hagadah*

Brombacher co-authored/illustrated, among others, *Meetings with Remarkable Souls* (Rabbi E. Klein), *The Light and Fire of the Baal Shem Tov* (Yitzhak Buxbaum), *When the Shouting Began* (S. Sher), *Letters of Light* (Rabbi A. Raskin), *I See Only Light* (S. Brombacher, H. Hamburger), *Holy Eating* (R. Schwartz, S. Brombacher), *Serach* (S. Brombacher, Y. Buxbaum), *Theophanie* (C. Zaffora), *Under the Chuppah, A Jewish Couple's Guide to Weddings and Meaningful Marriage* (S. Brombacher, Rabbi B. Forman), *Smokescreen* (Rabbi B. Forman, S. Brombacher), *A New Oracle of Kabbalah: Mystical Teachings of the Hebrew Letters: For Insight, Perspective, and Guidance* (R. Seidman, S. Brombacher), *Le Confessioni di Abulafia* (C. Zaffora, 2019), *On One Foot. The Life of Hillel. (*S. Brombacher, D. Zaklikowsky), *Rebbe Nachman's Tales: Stories for Personal Refinement.* (Rabbi B. Forman, S. Brombacher), *Inspired. Rosh Hashanah Prayer Companion.* (Rabbi Ch. Dalfin, S. Brombacher et al. ed. Chava Witkes)
Brombacher is currently working on: *Avraham Abulafia's Seven Paths of the Torah Seen through the yes of an artist. An artist synchresis of a 13th century kabbalistic text and its visual interpretation by a modern artist.* (publishing was postponed due to Covid related delays at the publishing house).

www.ingramcontent.com/pod-product-compliance
Lightning Source LLC
Chambersburg PA
CBHW040832040426
42336CB00034B/3458